IPSWICH

THE PHOTOGRAPHIC COLLECTION

These gentlemen are members of the Ipswich Photographic Society on an outing to Flatford in around 1890. Their elegant clothes and formal pose were captured on glass plate film in front of Willy Lot's Cottage, a famous feature of John Constable's *The Haywain*, painted around seventy years before this photograph was taken. We owe much to men like these, who toured around with their heavy plate cameras and wooden tripods, capturing life on film for later generations to enjoy. Photography did not become practical for the amateur until dry plate film became available in the 1870s. Before then photographers had to make their own film at the scene, then expose and develop it before it was dry (wet plate photography). This excluded most amateurs, and even the professionals tended to work in the studio, as taking water, chemicals, sheets of glass, and a portable darkroom to the scene was quite a task. In 1888 American George Eastman formed the Kodak company and marketed the roll-film box camera, bringing photography to all who could afford it.

IPSWICH

THE PHOTOGRAPHIC COLLECTION

DAVID KINDRED

SUTTON PUBLISHING LIMITED

This edition first published in 2003 by
Sutton Publishing Limited • Phoenix Mill
Thrupp • Stroud • Gloucestershire • GL5 2BU

Ipswich: A Second Selection was first published in 1993 by Alan Sutton Publishing Limited
Ipswich Revisited was first published in 1996 by Sutton Publishing Limited

British Library Cataloguing in Publication Data
A catalogue record for this book is available from the British Library.

ISBN 0 7509 3359 3

Typeset in 10.5/13.5 Photina.
Typesetting and origination by
Sutton Publishing Limited.
Printed and bound in England by
J.H. Haynes & Co. Ltd, Sparkford.

CONTENTS

PART ONE

IPSWICH

A dear old couple, more part of the nineteenth than the twentieth century, stand proudly outside their cottage in the late 1920s. This picture, taken on a half plate (6½ x 4¾ in) glass negative by Ipswich photographers, the Titshall Brothers, who toured the region with their wooden plate camera, captures an age gone forever. (Titshall Brothers)

INTRODUCTION

This selection of photographs from my collection, gathered over recent years, captures more of the historical life of Ipswich through the camera lens. The camera has provided an accurate record of life since the middle of the nineteenth century, photography recording more detail of life in the past than any other medium, but fashion in photography dictates that the record we have is patchy. In the period between 1860 and 1900 there are many studio portraits, as the fashion to have the family photographed, led by Queen Victoria, spread, but there are relatively few street scenes as technical obstacles kept most of the cameramen in the studio. The town itself is well recorded during the heyday of the postcard photographer, 1900–20, when everything – tourist views of the town, side streets and events – was marketed on postcard prints.

However, some of the biggest gaps in the photographic record are in the 1920–60 period. Recording the changes to the town was of little interest during the economic hard times of the late '20s and '30s. The war years saw restrictions on photography, as pictures of bomb damage could be valuable information to the enemy, helping them determine the accuracy of bombing raids. The shortage of film and other priorities meant little was recorded. A unique set of pictures which I discovered in 1992 of damage to the town is included in 'The War Years' section. It is difficult for those, like myself, born after the Second World War, to imagine life in the town with bombs raining down from the sky. The dock and the town's rail links put Ipswich on the German bombers' map.

Few pictures exist of the slum clearances of the 1950s and early '60s. Large areas were cleared, including the present site of Suffolk College (which was opened by the Queen in 1961), and much of the housing in the Stoke area of town. Little of life in these and similar parts of the town is recorded on film. Fortunately, we are more conscious nowadays of the need to record photographically.

There are a few names that surface every time research is done into the history of local topographical photography. Artist Robert Burrows was one of the first to take photographs of the town. A directory of 1858 has him registered as a photographer operating from premises near St Stephen's church. Wealthy philanthropist Richard Dykes Alexander, who lived in the large house at the Barrack Corner end of St Matthews Street, was another pioneering cameraman during the 1850s. William Vick operated from his studio at the corner of London Road and Clarkson Street from around 1870 to the late 1890s, and Harry Walters from the mid-1890s to the 1920s from his studios at 11 St Margarets Plain. The work of Ipswich photographers the Titshall Brothers, who worked from a small shop at 436 Spring Road, is featured.

Their unique record of life in the 1920s and '30s has an earthy charm and pictures 'real people' hard at work.

The importance of the amateur cameraman in filling many of the gaps should not be underestimated. Much of the work on file was by the amateur. Street scenes and events were recorded and filed by the likes of Mr W.C.S. 'Charlie' Girling. He took pictures from the late 1920s, and was recording changes until his death in late 1991.

Burrows and Alexander were taking pictures of the town when Charles Dickens visited Ipswich for a week, a visit he wrote about in the magazine *All Year Round* of 1 October 1859. The article gives some idea of life in the town at that time as seen through the eyes of the famous writer. He travelled up the River Orwell by ferry from Harwich. 'As you quit the landing stage and enter the town you come to one irregular street after another; curves abound, pathways are narrow and the old fashioned houses are not merely dotted about, but you may walk under a series of projecting first floors as you please and feast your eyes on infinite gables . . . After wandering about for some time you will probably find yourself on the Cornhill, a very large square in which the Corn Exchange and Town Hall are conspicuous buildings . . . Perceiving that the streets were very intricate, I lost no time in inquiring for a map of Ipswich and its environs and for an Ipswich guide . . . A map was not to be obtained. One had indeed been published in 1840 but it was out of print and you could not get a copy for love nor money. [He was able to buy a guide by J. Witherspoon published some years earlier.] What renders J. Witherspoon's book of peculiar excitement is the circumstances that it was published in 1842, about 17 years ago, and since that time vandalic hands have made rather free with the antiquities of Ipswich. Hence when he tells you that some prime curiosity is to be found in such a nook, and when by dint of a deal of inquiry you reach the nook in question, it is by no means certain that you will find the curiosity.'

Dickens was enchanted by the Ancient House and described in detail the exterior of this 'old house'. He also comments on the fine carved corner post of the Half Moon Inn at the corner of Lower Brook Street and Foundation Street.

His stay included visits to several taverns, including the Royal Oak in Northgate Street, the Neptune in Fore Street and the Tankard in Tacket Street. He took a steamboat ride to Harwich, he thought 'at a price ridiculously low', and fished on the River Gipping. As he set off for London a fellow traveller asked Dickens if he had enjoyed the Arboretum; he admitted he had not seen the splendid floral arena. '"Then", ejaculated my fellow traveller, "you have missed the best thing in Ipswich."' What a pity Dickens did not take an interest in the new science of photography. What a fascinating set of photographs that would have been!

I have arranged the book so that pictures are grouped together in themes. Inevitably, several pictures fall into more than one category. For example, photographers seem to have had a fascination for the town's trams. Many street scenes feature a tram so they crop up both in the general section on the town and in the transport pages.

David Kindred

CHAPTER ONE

THE BOROUGH OF IPSWICH

The first section of the book looks at some of the many changes the town has seen, and includes photographs from 1859 through to the mid-1960s. There are pictures of events, incidents, firemen, shops, schools and public houses, all of which help make up the character of a town.

Tavern Street, looking towards Carr Street, around 1910. Frederick Fish's Suffolk House store, 'Merchant Drapers and House Furnishers', is in the middle of the picture.

This picture by pioneer Ipswich photographer Robert Burrows was taken in 1859 when the Woolpack was a public house on the edge of town. Robert Burrows is better known as an artist than a photographer. He worked as a young man in the family silversmith business in Ipswich but his skills as a landscape artist set him on a new career. In 1850 he took a keen interest in the new science of photography. The town is lucky to still have some of his fine landscapes and his original photographs. The sign in the picture offers 'Rum and milk every morning'. Only a tiny cottage stands in Westerfield Road where a row of houses is today.

A view of the Westerfield Road–Tuddenham Road junction from Bolton Lane around 1910. The scene has changed dramatically in the fifty or so years since the picture opposite was taken, although little has changed since.

The rear yard of the Golden Lion Hotel in the 1890s. This view of the stables from Lion Street, close to the town centre, is still recognizable today.

A group of Victorian figures pose for the camera by one of Ipswich's famous sights, Wolsey's Gate in College Street. The gate, with Henry VIII's royal arms above, is all that remains of the great seat of learning that Cardinal Wolsey planned for Ipswich, the town of his birth. Work that had been started was demolished and the King had the building material taken to London.

Great Colman Street in 1965, with the furniture store of John Blundle on the right. Sketchley, the cleaners, occupied the building facing the camera at this time. This building started as the town's Assembly Rooms in 1821, but later became a school of art. In 1878 the Ipswich High School for Girls was established in the building, but that moved to Westerfield Road in 1907. Egerton's motor engineering works, Sketchley, and a stationery shop have operated from here since then. (Terry Neeves)

A Victorian view of the building in Northgate Street featured in the picture above. A second floor and shop window were later added to this once-columned building. (William Vick)

This building in Princes Street was known as the 'Grasshopper' from an emblem that once hung on it. Barclays Bank now stands on the site. The building on the left edge of the picture was then the Corn Exchange, demolished to make way for the post office which opened in 1881. In the period just before its closure, the 'Grasshopper' was a grocers shop. (William Vick)

The Ipswich Working Girls' Club and Restaurant at 39 Carr Street in the early 1890s. On the left is W.J. Curtis' hairdressers shop. Neither of these premises, which were close to the Salutation public house, remains today. (William Vick)

The Provincial Dyeing and Cleaning Company at 29 Carr Street in 1915. Its advertisement said, 'Ladies costumes cleaned and dyed at shortest notice'. The shop was next to the gas showrooms which can just be seen on the left.

The *East Anglian Daily Times* first appeared on 13 October 1874. The paper was then published from 21 Upper Brook Street. The *Star* was first published by the company in 1885. In 1887 the company moved to 13 Carr Street, pictured above, and operated from this fine Victorian building until a move to new premises in Lower Brook Street in 1966. Sadly, this building was lost to the town with the redevelopment of the site for the Eastgate Shopping Centre. The road to the left of the building was Little Colman Street; there is still a way from Carr Street to Great Colman Street through the shopping centre at this point. This photograph must have been taken when the buildings opposite were redeveloped in 1888. (William Vick)

A Victorian view of Carr Street from White Horse Corner. This view from around 1890 features the lines for the horse-drawn trams and the *East Anglian Daily Times* Company's premises. (William Vick)

Carr Street from where Woolworths store is today, looking towards White Horse Corner. On the right is the Lyceum Theatre, which closed in 1936 to be replaced by the Great Universal Stores of Manchester. The site is now part of the Eastgate Shopping Centre.

Fuller's shop in Upper Brook Street in the early 1890s. The shop sign advertises Fuller's hand-welted boots. These fine old buildings were close to White Horse Corner. (William Vick)

Upper Brook Street from Northgate Street around 1912. The buildings on the opposite page can be seen on the left of the picture, next to Paviour and Company's drapery store.

The Fox Inn in Upper Brook Street around 1905. The two boys on the left are standing where the door to Sainsburys is now.

The Ancient House in the Buttermarket was built in the fifteenth century. The royal arms on the front of the building are those of Charles II. The building on the left is the Wagon and Horses Inn, later the site of the Ritz Cinema (later renamed the ABC), which was in turn demolished to become part of the Buttermarket Shopping Centre. The buildings on the north side between Dial Lane and Princes Street, including Wrinch's 'Furnishing Ironmongers', were rebuilt at the turn of the century in order to facilitate widening of the road. This picture by Robert Burrows was taken in the late 1850s.

ST. LAWRENCE CHURCH, IPSWICH.

BUTTER MARKET

25 KEEBL

St Lawrence church and Dial Lane from St Stephens Lane around 1906.

The Buttermarket from the Upper Brook Street end in the late 1870s. The left-hand side has changed drastically since this picture was taken. Fire destroyed the building on the left on 2 August 1992, then Hughes' electrical store. The shop next door, just off the left of the picture, Alderton's shoe shop, was also destroyed. The loss of these buildings was a sad blow. The Hughes building was the only three-jetty timber-framed building left in the town. Alderton's shoe shop was another timber-framed building with a Georgian façade. The site between the scene of the 1992 fire and the Ancient House is now part of the Buttermarket Shopping Centre. Part of this site was previously the Ritz Cinema. A street directory of the late 1870s shows that on the left side of the street was the Wagon and Horses, at No. 32 (next to the Ancient House). This public house had stood on the site from the mid-sixteenth century. From here a wagon made a weekly departure to London; stables stood behind the building until the 1920s. The Wagon and Horses was demolished in the 1930s when the cinema was built on the site. Oliver Staines, printer, was at No. 34; John Orton and Co., ironmongers, had Nos 36 and 38; Phillips and Piper were at No. 40 (with the lamp over the door), with Mrs Sarah Phillips living above the premises; Joseph Thurston, cabinet-maker, was at No. 42, where Hughes' shop was; Thomas Alderton, boot manufacturers and forerunners of the shop that burned down, were at No. 44.

A busy Buttermarket from the Princes Street end on 28 January 1949, with a two-way flow of traffic. The left side of this view has altered little, although on the right side of the street the Buttermarket Shopping Centre has greatly changed the scene. The Buttermarket in the mid-nineteenth century was a narrow lane paved with cobblestones. Between St Lawrence Lane and Upper Brook Street the upper floors of the houses were so close that people could almost shake hands from the windows. (Howard Studios)

The Buttermarket from Upper Brook Street around 1950.

This pair of inns, the Sickle (left) and Kings Head, at the corner of King Street and Princes Street, was photographed in 1878, shortly before being sold as lots. They were demolished the following year to make way for the new Corn Exchange which opened on 26 July 1882, when the mayor, Mr Frederick Fish, held a dinner for 600 people to celebrate the occasion. The rear of the Town Hall is on the right of the picture. (William Vick)

Westgate Street, looking towards the Cornhill, in the 1930s, with (from the right) Jays furniture shop, Lambert's tobacconists, Howard's photographic studio, and the public hall which was destroyed by fire on 26 February 1948. The fire was first noticed by police sergeant J. Mann at 6.15 a.m. but soon spread through the building. It was thought to have started in the restaurant at the rear of the building. (Percy Chinery)

A sea of faces in the public hall in 1928. The event was part of the celebrations for the Ipswich Co-operative Society's sixtieth anniversary.

A busy Westgate Street on 28 January 1949. The flow of traffic was then both ways. One of the town's trolleybuses is heading towards the Cornhill past Footman Pretty's Waterloo House store (now Debenhams). A huge clock hangs outside H. Samuel's shop on the right. Next door a sign in the window of Easiephit says, 'All footwear now coupon free', a sign that rationing, started in wartime, was coming to an end. (Howard Studios)

Three of Ipswich's electric trams are included in this view of the Cornhill from around 1905, with cabmen waiting in the foreground for customers. The taxi service was removed from the Cornhill when Lloyds Avenue opened on 5 January 1930.

A view similar to that above, taken around ten years later. The Boer War memorial in the foreground was unveiled on the Cornhill on 29 September 1906. It now stands in Christchurch Park. The cabs were mostly motorized by this time, although the drinking trough for the horses was not taken away until 1928.

Christchurch Mansion covered in ivy in a postcard view by Harry Walters from around 1900.

Christ's Hospital School in Wherstead Road stood between Purplett Street and Tyler Street. The school was founded after Nicholas Phillips, a portman of the town, bequeathed a farm at Debenham in 1670 so that the profits could be devoted to the education of poor children. The school continued until 1883, when its endowments were merged with Ipswich School. (William Vick)

St Margarets Street from Majors Corner around 1912. Everything in this photograph has gone; all of the attractive little shops and dwellings having been demolished. This once thriving part of town included the premises of William Cooper, 'Dealers in Antiques' (right). The Mulberry Tree pub at the junction of Woodbridge Road is in the centre of the picture. This was rebuilt, set further back, in the late 1920s. The Odeon Cinema now stands on the right of this view.

St Nicholas Street has largely survived the changes to the town centre and still looks much as it did in this postcard picture from around 1910. The shop on the left, at the corner of Cromwell Street (now Cromwell Square), was G. Siegwart, watchmaker and jeweller.

The Engineers Arms in Bath Street was aptly named, being so close to the engineering works of Ransomes and Rapier. This picture was taken on 30 December 1948.

The interior of the Ipswich Working Men's College at 21 Tavern Street. Hunter's *Handbook of Ipswich* of 1864 describes the college: 'A new but excellent educational society which has hitherto been located in rooms at the Town Hall which will shortly be removed to the old assembly rooms in Tower Street.' The entrance to the college was in Tavern Street, close to the corner with Tower Street. The college closed early in the twentieth century. (William Vick)

Tavern Street in the early 1880s. This picture, by William Vick, was taken from about where the entrance to the Tower Ramparts Shopping Centre is, looking towards White Horse Corner. A directory of the period lists the shops on the right of the street as, from the right: No. 12, Lewis Brothers, drapers; No. 14, Cornel and Cornel, chemists and druggists; No. 16, William Bennet, grocer; Nos 18–20, Frederick Corder, linen draper; No. 22, John Wagstaff, hatter; No. 24–6 Meadow and Bennett, furnishing and general ironmonger; No. 28, William Hunt, bookseller and fancy stationer; No. 30, J. Driver, milliner and lace depot; No. 32, J. Buckingham and Son, boot and shoe manufacturer; Nos 34–8, Thompson Wilson, pastry cook and confectioner. An interesting mix of trades for the Victorian shopper.

The premises of Frank Mason and Son Ltd, drapers, at the corner of Tavern Street and Tower Street in the late 1920s. The building stands on the site of numerous old taverns, from which Tavern Street took its name. Mr Frank Mason was apprenticed to Frederick Fish and Son, a general store in Tavern Street (see p. 11), where he identified a need for a 'ladies' shop'. In 1899 he took over the corner site known as the London Bazaar. In 1903 he extended to No. 17 Tavern Street, a furriers business run by a Miss Bowen. In 1928 No. 15a was absorbed, and the title of the firm changed to Frank Mason and Son when Mr Mason's son Geoffrey joined the business. The building still stands on the corner, although Mason's closed in 1970.

Fashion at Mason's Tavern Street store from the turn of the twentieth century, with elegant clothes set out for the camera.

Parasols and petticoats were among the items for sale at Mason's.

An Edwardian view of the Great White Horse Hotel and Tavern Street. A policeman controls the traffic at the junction of Northgate Street, Carr Street, Upper Brook Street and Tavern Street. The first automatic signals in Ipswich were installed at the junction on 20 November 1929. Traffic lights came into use at Majors Corner on 2 December in the same year.

Tavern Street in December 1965. Frederick Corder's store on the left has since gone, having been redeveloped into smaller units. On the right of the street were Richard's clothes shop, Joe Lyons Restaurant, and the Stead and Simpson and Mansfield shoe shops. The entrance to the Tower Ramparts Shopping Centre is now where Lyons Restaurant stood. (Terry Neeves)

Tavern Street from Carr Street on 5 September 1967, with J. J. Edwards' shop on the right of the street. Edwards' shop is remembered with affection by the generations which, as children, visited with their parents to be fitted with school uniforms.

The old Manor House on St Margarets Green, a seventeenth-century former merchant's house photographed around 1905. Local character Margaret Catchpole worked as a servant here for the Cobbold family in the 1790s. The neighbouring Manor Ballroom was modernized in 1991, but the old house is largely intact.

Early in the twentieth century a new water reservoir was built in Park Road to cope with the town's increased need for clean water. The reservoir, capable of holding four and a half million gallons of water, was constructed by Mr George Bell of Tottenham from plans made by the borough engineer, Mr Hamlet Roberts, at a cost of just under £20,000. The reservoir was photographed before being roofed in. It has 375 cast-iron columns supporting one and a half miles of steel joists, on which rests a roof of 6,829 sq yd.

Stoke Bridge is now one of the busiest through routes in Ipswich, the flow of traffic making it difficult to cross the road. At the time of this photograph, in the 1920s, however, these two young boys were able to linger in the road. This bridge opened in 1925, to replace the iron bridge built in 1819.

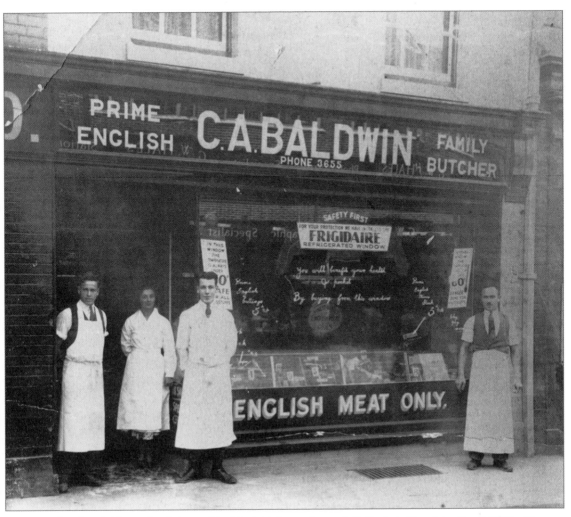

Mr Charles Baldwin (right) outside his butchers shop at 8 Tacket Street in the 1930s. Mr Baldwin claimed to have the first refrigerated window in town. The notices in the window proclaim the advantages of the Frigidaire slab. 'Safety first. For your protection we now have a refrigerated window'. A handwritten sign underneath has the slogan, 'You will benefit your health and pocket by buying from this window'. English meat is advertised at 5d per pound. Mrs Nora Baldwin is in the doorway of the shop between two assistants.

A promotional cart belonging to Talbot and Company, mineral water manufacturers, whose works were in St Georges Street. On the cart is a giant version of the company's stone ginger beer bottles. The picture is from around 1912.

Fore Street, with the Neptune Inn on the left, in a postcard view of around 1908. This picture was taken from near the end of what is now Grimwade Street (but was then Church Street), looking towards the town centre.

The Sea Horse stood at the junction of College Street and Foundation Street. It closed in the mid-1970s and was demolished as part of a road improvement scheme.

A marching band in St Matthews Street for the Labour Day procession of 1933. Revett's motorcycle and light car showroom and R. Deeks' milliners shop are in the background. (W.C.S. Girling)

Established in 1851, Phillips and Piper Ltd was a specialist in high-grade 'ready for service' clothing. Its factory had frontages on St Margarets Street and Old Foundry Road, and employed up to 600 people. The company's largely female staff made clothing under the 'Lambourne' label, including sportswear, suits, overcoats, and 'Pytchley' riding breeches and pantaloons. This picture of 1934 was taken in a packed number one machine room. The building has been converted into flats and is now called Pipers Court.

A pony pulls a buggy past The Boar's Head, a Cobbold public house in Boar's Head Lane. This part of town, which has undergone redevelopment, is near to Stoke Bridge.

The Rising Sun, at the corner of Princes Street and James Street, in July 1948. St Clare House now stands close to this site.

The Happy Return was at the corner of Albion Street and Holywells Road. Men from the nearby gasworks and dock, and from Ransomes, Sims and Jefferies would have kept the landlord, Mr A. Botwright, busy in October 1948 when this picture was taken.

Teachers and pupils of the Ipswich Central Council School in Smart Street around 1907. The school had facilities for 350 boys and 380 girls. The boys department had lessons in workshop, commercial courses and typewriting, while the girls were taught cooking, laundry, dressmaking, shorthand, typewriting and commercial work.

The Union flag flutters in the breeze as pupils line up outside the Ipswich Central Council School in 1907.

Pupils in the main hall of Bramford Road Infants School in 1928. The original of this picture belongs to Stan Calvesbert of Moore Road, Ipswich. With remarkable memory, he recalls the names of Reggie Parker, Russell Cobb, ? Kitson, ? Dennis, ? Nice, Ronald Green, Henry Podd, the Page brothers, Kenny Laflin, Ronnie Welham, ? Ager, Basil Warren, Charlie Last, Jackie Edwards, ? Fenton and ? Mayhew. Stan is standing on the extreme left of the picture. The old school building at the corner of Bramford Road and Gatacre Road is now shared by Suffolk Record Office and the Sir John Mills Theatre.

An aerial view of Northgate School in the early 1930s. A brochure published at the time says the 'provision made by the education committee of the corporation for secondary education in Ipswich may be said to be a model of its kind, and those who would put this claim to the acid test are invited to inspect the recently opened Northgate School, in which the old Municipal Secondary School for boys and the Municipal Secondary for girls have been, so to speak, separately united'. The school, extensively rebuilt and improved, is now a mixed high school. The site includes one of the town's sports centres.

Wellington Stores was on the corner of Waterloo Road and Wellington Street. This picture, from around 1908, shows the Calvesbert family, Charles (left), Annette (Nettie), Bertie (right), and their mother Ellen, who ran the shop from around 1883 to 1913. The shop sold a great variety of goods, from corn to shoe polish, cycle spares to cold rice pudding! The window display includes jars of sweets, vegetables, and a sign advertising 'new and skim milk'.

A huge blaze destroyed buildings on a site bounded by Norwich Road, Waterloo Road and Wellington Street on 21 January 1909. At about 10 p.m. Mr Calvesbert, who ran the shop at the corner of Waterloo Road, smelt burning but on checking outside found nothing and went to bed. About half an hour later he was woken by shouts of 'Fire'. Burning buildings belonging to local builders were threatening nearby housing. Part of a report in the *Evening Star* the following day said, 'By this time the whole neighbourhood was in a turmoil, and excitement was tremendous. By 11.30 the whole of the three cornered area was a seething mass of blazing timber with their sparks and immense clouds of golden smoke which converted the scene into a brilliant spectacle such as has seldom been surpassed in Ipswich on such terrible occasions.' One of the burning buildings was a stable, and three horses were trapped by the blaze. A quick-thinking gang of men smashed a hole in the back wall of the stables and led the panicking animals to safety.

The hole in the stable wall in Wellington Street, through which the horses were rescued.

The rescued horses after the drama of the night before.

Brass-helmeted Ipswich firemen line up on St Margarets Green for the United Friendly Society's
Hospital Sunday on 25 September 1912. Hospital Sunday was an annual fund-raising event
with a carnival-style parade through town. The parades began in 1894 and were held until
1937. In that period almost £6,000 was donated to the Ipswich and East Suffolk Hospital.

The town's firemen using their brass helmets for coin collection at the Hospital Sunday of 1911.

The familiar three-balled sign of the pawnbroker hangs from the corner of R.D. and J.B. Fraser's building in Elm Street in this picture from around 1870. The furnishing business of Frasers (Ipswich) Ltd grew from these small beginnings.

This fine R.D. and J.B. Fraser building stood at the corner of Princes Street and Museum Street. It was built in 1890, replacing the offices of the *Ipswich Journal* newspaper that had occupied the site since 1866. In April 1912 the building was totally destroyed by fire. It was rebuilt in similar style. The building has since been converted into offices. (Harry Walters)

A crowd gathers in Museum Street to view the remains of Fraser's store. The Black Bell Inn, now demolished, can be seen at the corner of Elm Street.

Rubble blocks Museum Street after the fire at Fraser's store in April 1912.

In 1830 the protection of Ipswich against fire was in the hands of the Suffolk Alliance Fire Office, which maintained two large and three small manual pumps, one kept by the police. The service was staffed by a superintendent, Mr Bruce Pyman, whose duties were part time, for which he was paid £20 per year, and twenty-eight men, 'aided at big conflagrations by men who were naturally attracted to the scene'. On 9 November 1875 the Town Council decided to take over the service and formed a fire brigade separate from the police force. It had been common in many towns for the police to operate the fire service. The brigade was housed in Waterworks Street. On 28 January 1876 Mr W. Wheeler, 'a breezy sailor', was appointed superintendent. On 21 February 1884 the first horse-drawn steampump arrived; a second steampump followed in June 1899. These machines served the town until the 1920s. With the growth of the service and its equipment, new housing was needed and the brigade moved to Bond Street on 13 November 1899. The equipment consisted of the two steamers, a first aid machine, two of the old manual pumps and three hose trucks. In February 1918 a Ford motor tender was added and in 1920 the horses were done away with. The picture shows one of the horse-drawn pumps leaving the Bond Street Fire Station, the brass-helmeted firemen dashing to a 'shout' around 1916.

A huge fire destroyed premises in Princes Street on 22 February 1950, causing an estimated £100,000 worth of damage. The fire started in the premises of Haddock and Baines, paper merchants and printers, and soon spread to the neighbouring Central Cinema (in the middle of the picture). Projectionist Mr O. Driscoll was in the middle of changing the feature films *The Dolly Sisters* starring Betty Grable and *Call North Side 777* with James Stewart. Manager Mr J.H. Baker cleared the audience of three hundred as the fire raged through the building. The fire brigade, who fought the inferno with Second World War tenders and trailer pumps, called men and equipment from Holbrook, Hadleigh, Needham Market, Woodbridge and Colchester to assist. The buildings were gutted by the blaze. A crowd of onlookers can just be seen watching from the end of Princes Street, with Barclays Bank behind them. (Henry Clarke)

Hubert's cycle shop at 180 Felixstowe Road, opposite the Royal Oak, in 1915. Signs in the window advertise Osram lamps, Lodge plugs, Pratt's Spirit and the Cyclonier puncture remedy. The shop has been a Laundromat in recent years; the post office next door has survived.

By 1932 Hubert's business had moved to 289 Felixstowe Road and expanded into motor engineering, with a set of pumps selling Cleveland Petrol at 1s 2d per gallon.

The Feathers Hotel at the corner of Westgate Street and Lady Lane in 1949. The *Evening Star* reported in June 1967, 'Masonry of the old west gate of Ipswich was uncovered in Westgate Street on the site of the now demolished Feathers pub. The bottom of the wall, which was uncovered during demolition and reconstruction work, is ten feet below the present road level.'

The Crown, another of the public houses that stood close to Ipswich Dock. At the corner of Bridge Street and Greyfriars Road, the site is now part of the roundabout system near Stoke Bridge. This photograph was taken in October 1948 when Mr H. Jessup was the landlord.

The tiny terraced houses, with outside toilets, in Wells Street were demolished in February 1956 to make way for the flats of Wells Court.

The walls of Wells Street come crashing to the ground on 7 February 1956.

A view from the roof of William Pretty's factory in Crown Street on 10 August 1966, giving a panoramic view of demolition work on town centre housing. The terraced housing of Charles Street, Beck Street, Fitzroy Street (with parked vehicles), Chenery Street and Peel Street is being reduced to rubble. This once densely populated area is now occupied by Crown House offices, Crown car park and Crown Pools.

The houses of Beck Street being demolished in August 1966.

The Ostrich Inn near Bourne Bridge around 1900. The inn has stood on this site since the early seventeenth century.

Crowds cheer and flags flutter in the summer breeze for the visit of Queen Mary to Ipswich on 14 June 1938. The royal limousine is driving along St Margarets Plain, with the buildings of Fonnereau Road in the background. The bakers shop, on the extreme left of the picture, was demolished in the late 1940s as part of a road-widening scheme. (Harry Walters)

Norwich Road, *c.* 1900. The Christmas stock of William Rush of 46 Norwich Road is displayed on the front of the building and on trestle tables on the pavement. A sign on the side wall advertises 'Ice Importer', a luxury in the days before homes had refrigeration.

The Steam Packet Inn, Duke Street, October 1948. This picture was taken from where the Duke Street–Fore Street roundabout now is. The Steam Packet closed around 1950.

A. Chambers' shop and off-licence at the corner of Dales Road and Dale Hall Lane, photographed on 17 January 1949. The Dales public house now stands on this corner.

A busy scene at the crossroads of Albion Street (left), Cavendish Street (with the advertising board on the side of the house) and Fore Hamlet in the late 1940s, as cyclists start to pedal hard for the climb up Bishops Hill. On the right is a tiny shop advertising the sale of Will's Woodbine cigarettes and Brooke Bond tea. Most of the buildings in this view have been demolished in road-widening and improvement schemes.

Bunting decorates the terraced houses of Albion Street for the Silver Jubilee celebrations of King George V on 6 May 1935. Keen amateur photographer Mr 'Charlie' Girling toured the town recording the events of the day, and on this and the next page are some of the results of his work. Albion Street ran from the bottom of Bishops Hill to where Duke Street is now. The celebration was typical of street parties held all over town to mark this royal occasion. There was a procession through the town centre, and huge beacons were lit at Whitton and at the airport. In 1936 the King died. On the day of his funeral everybody left work at noon so they could listen to the service on the 'wireless'. With most workers using cycles, Mr Girling remembers that the junction of Fore Street and Salthouse Street 'was so congested with cycles it was impossible to fall off'!

Crowds gather at Barrack Corner for the Silver Jubilee parade. One of the town's single-deck trolleybuses passes George Moore's drapery store and Daniel's piano shop. (W.C.S. Girling)

Crowds pack Westgate Street for the King George V Jubilee celebration procession of 6 May 1935. A picture from the St Matthews Street end, looking towards the Cornhill. (W.C.S. Girling)

Buildings in St Margarets Street smothered in flags for the Prince of Wales' visit to the town in June 1930. The businesses were, from the left: William Olley, fruiterer, George Clarke, fishmonger, E.J. Gould, pork butcher, John Sadd, hairdresser, and Fred Carr, bootmaker. (Titshall Brothers)

The St John's Orphanage stood at the corner of Bloomfield Street and Freehold Road, and by all accounts was a grim place for the poor young souls who were placed in care there. When the children first arrived they were stripped, bathed, examined and given a very short haircut, recalled Mr Henry Webb in a letter to the *Evening Star*'s 'Way We Were' column in February 1992. Mr Webb, who lived with his brother at the home for eight years in the 1930s, remembers how a former Army sergeant with a huge waxed moustache greeted them for years of strict discipline, routine and daily tasks. 'Life in St John's was very regimental. Good hidings fell like rain. Other forms of punishment were always at hand if one was adjudged to have done wrong. Early to bed without tea, or extra tasks. The officers, nearly all ex-Army sergeants, treated the children like Army privates. The day started at 6 a.m. with a dash downstairs for a strip wash in a basin in near cold water in the outside washhouse. After a breakfast of stodgy porridge, one thick slice of bread and marg and a mug of tea the children would perform tasks before school. Evening work involved scrubbing floors, six boys in line kneeling with pail and scrubbers. Saturdays always started with a large dose of "opening medicine" before going down to the washhouse. Later this would take effect and a long fidgety queue to the outside doorless row of cold-seated toilets would stretch across the yard.' Mr Webb added, 'Life was hard at St John's but we never absconded. We were too damn scared to even think about it!' The picture shows the staff of the home in 1907.

Celebration in Little Barclay Street for the coronation of George VI on 12 May 1937. The tiny street is packed with residents and others from the area. Bunting was strung from the houses as children sat at the tables for a celebration tea. The houses of Little Barclay Street, Permit Office Street, Barclay Street and Cox Lane were cleared when residents were moved out about two years after this picture was taken, mostly to the new Whitton estate.

Another view of the party in Little Barclay Street. After the party the children were sent home with a bag containing sweets, an apple, an orange and a new penny.

The Co-op store in Vernon Street in the mid-1920s, with manager Harry Wyatt at the door. The shop was the first one opened after the Carr Street store had started trading. The window displays urge customers to 'Buy within the Empire'.

A postcard view of Bramford Road around 1910, with Holder's newsagents on the corner of Rendlesham Road on the left.

Residents and staff of Tooley's Court in the grounds of the homes in Foundation Street around 1900. Henry Tooley provided money to build almshouses in the town when he died in 1551, leaving the greater part of his wealth to the Corporation to provide homes for the elderly poor, preferably old soldiers. The original building near the old Shire Hall became the foundation, which in turn gave Foundation Street its name. Nearly half a century later Ipswich merchant William Smart added to Tooley's legacy and Tooley's and Smart's Almshouses were run as the Ipswich Municipal Charities until 1835, when the administration was transferred to trustees. The homes are now known as Tooley's Court and the complex is administered by trustees under Ipswich Foundation Street Charities.

The Ipswich area was hit by flooding on 25 January 1939 when the River Gipping burst its banks. Much of Ipswich was swamped by the flood, homes were abandoned, and people took to rowing boats for transport. Damage was estimated at 'thousands of pounds', although the exact figure was never known. Amazingly, only one person was killed. A lethal combination of melting snow and heavy rain proved too much for the Gipping valley. Within hours it was transformed into a huge lake. Roads, railways and telephone lines were rendered useless as the flood tide rose. In Ipswich, families were marooned in their homes without food, water or fires. Hundreds of homes were ruined. The first sign of disaster came at midnight when the river level started to rise. Three hours later the water was pouring from Whitton and settling in the Dales Road area. Properties in the Beaconsfield Road and Yarmouth Road area were badly affected, and at 3.55 p.m. the Gipping burst its banks at the London Road Bridge. Over the weekend the water subsided and the mopping up operation began. The picture shows flood water in Princes Street (looking towards the station). The Princes Street roundabout is now where this picture was taken from, with Civic Drive off to the right.

A lorry creates a wave of water in Bridge Street. Stoke Bridge can just be seen in the distance. This was the only open route to the south from the town.

Another view of Bridge Street, with a truck from Myrtle House Laundry of Schreiber Road making its way to Stoke Bridge.

Water pouring back into the river near Stoke Bridge.

A pedestrian watches as a car makes its way slowly through the flood water at London Road near the Ipswich Arms public house.

An aerial view of the bridge over the River Gipping at Bramford, which was swept away by the flood.

Sightseers gather by the fallen bridge at Bramford. The view is taken from over the village.

Heavy summer rain brought flooding to St Helens Street on 26 July 1911. Shopkeepers are busy trying to prevent as much damage as they can as the water swirls down the street. The shop in the foreground, on the corner of Regent Street, is Henry Blackwell provision merchant, licensed to sell beer, wine and spirits. The shop next door is K. Blackwell's shop, selling fresh coffee. Fry's Chocolate is advertised in the window. These buildings remain much the same today.

Flat-capped human horses pull a float along London Road during the Holywells Labour Fête in 1933. Percy Chinery, who took this picture, entitled it 'Workers Hauling Capitalism'. In the background is Ranelagh Road School.

The Salvation Army band plays hymns in the summer sunshine in Broomhill Road on a Sunday in 1933. The sound of their brass instruments and drums would have been heard the length of the street in the days when most homes did not have even a simple radio set. (W.C.S. Girling)

A street since wiped from the map of Ipswich. This shows Wykes Bishop Street, with Alfred Bowell's church bell foundry in the right foreground. Wykes Bishop Street ran from Fore Hamlet to where Duke Street is now.

Members of the Stoke Guild Football Club proudly hold the trophy after a cup final replay in April 1920 with the Great Eastern Railway team at the Orwell Works Ground in Sidegate Lane. The Stoke team won 1–0 and its supporters were keen to join in the official team photograph.

The staff of H.C. Day's transport and removal company line up with their vehicles in the late 1930s. The company operated from 961 Woodbridge Road and 182 Britannia Road.

The Fountain Inn was at the corner of Myrtle Road and Holywells Road. This picture was taken in November 1948. The pub closed in the mid-1950s.

A man who did much to record changes in the town was photographer Harry Walters. He worked from his studio and home at 11 St Margarets Plain between the 1890s and the 1920s. He took thousands of portraits and family groups in his 'glass house' studio in the garden of his home (see opposite), and recorded much of the town in postcard views during the same period. Sadly, after his retirement his glass negatives were buried in the garden of the house and destroyed. This self portrait shows that he had a great sense of humour. Using trick photography, he sits in his garden, knife and fork in hand, with his own head on the bowl.

A view from the studio of photographer Harry Walters of his own family in the garden of their home at 11 St Margarets Plain around 1908. Harry Walters worked in a glass house studio to make full use of the daylight. His two daughters, Bertha and Winnie, each have a fine doll's pram, son Jack holds a wheelbarrow, and Mrs Walters looks on.

A flock of sheep on Christchurch Park help keep the grass short. This picture from early in the twentieth century was taken from near the Fonnereau Road entrance and looks towards the round pond.

J. Rush's bakery and confectionary at the corner of Woodbridge Road and Khartoum Road around 1912.

The Three Swans in Princes Street, at the corner with Cecilia Street, in January 1949. This was one of nine public houses that stood in Princes Street between the Cornhill and the railway station. The advertisement on the wall is for the Picture House in Tavern Street (see p. 130) where seats were 1s, 1s 9d, 2s 3d and 2s 9d. The film showing was *If You Knew Susie* with Eddie Cantor. On the right is Knight's tobacconists shop.

Christmas Day at the Heathfields Workhouse, 1952. This stern-looking institution was home for the less fortunate. Situated where the Ipswich hospital is now, it had an entrance lodge in Woodbridge Road. The home opened in 1899 to replace the Union Workhouse in Great Whip Street. The *Evening Star* reported the opening: 'Without going into dry details as to the internal arrangements of the new structure, suffice to say that the arrangements have been carried out with special regard to the comfort and convenience of the officials, and the sick and old, the object being that the Workhouse should be anything but a pleasant home for the drunken, immoral or lazy able-bodied.'

The Joiners Arms in Castle Street in January 1949. Castle Street was where the Civic Centre now stands.

Boy scouts help at the Ipswich Sanatorium open-air whist drive on 29 June 1910. The sanatorium was out of town on the Foxhall Road, close to where the speedway stadium is now. It was built by public subscription as a memorial to King Edward VII.

Northgate Street early in the century. The street has changed little since this picture was taken. The timber building at the corner of Oak Lane (left) was originally a fifteenth- or sixteenth-century house. It was used as an inn, the Royal Oak, in the middle of the nineteenth century, and converted back to something like the original merchant's house, with parts of other local buildings, around 1855. There was another inn of the same name in Tavern Street. The present Royal Oak is at the corner of Felixstowe Road and Derby Road.

The Ipswich Town Council, including the mayor, Mr A.C. Churchman, and town officials, on the steps of the Town Hall on the coronation day of King Edward VII, in 1902. The mayor provided tea for thousands of children in the town, and the day ended with a firework display.

A road repair team poses for the camera in Lower Brook Street around 1930. A pile of tar blocks provides a seat for one of the workmen and a group of schoolgirls has also got in on the photo session. The buildings in the background remain today. (Titshall Brothers)

The Griffin Inn at the corner of Bath Street and New Cut West was a popular pub with dock workers and employees of Ransomes and Rapiers, the nearby engineering works. The Griffin was photographed in June 1948, when Mr A. Crisp was the landlord; it closed in the early 1950s.

The beat of the drummers leads this Territorial Field Ambulance band as it marches along Chevallier Street during a church parade at All Saints' church in 1909. When this picture was taken Chevallier Street was just a side street connecting Bramford Road and Norwich Road. Yarmouth Road and Valley Road, which form the link today with this major through route, had not yet been built.

In the span of a single lifetime this scene has changed beyond recognition. Around seventy years separate the pictures on these facing pages. The Seven Arches Bridge carried traffic on the London Road across the River Orwell. The view above, by William Vick, shows a country scene, water flowing fast under the bridge while men and boys stand and watch on a winter day. The house on the distant left is the only sign of town life in this scene. In 1891 the town's population was 57,360 and the Seven Arches Bridge was a walk out of town. The bridge that has replaced this attractive structure now carries thousands of vehicles a day on the road between Hadleigh Road and Yarmouth Road roundabouts.

A sad end for the old bridge on the London Road, as demolition men break up the structure with pneumatic drills in May 1959.

The Half Moon Inn stood at the corner of Lower Brook Street and Foundation Street. It was demolished in 1959. It was one of the town's oldest buildings and had a fine carved corner post. There was a sign on the building which read, 'The carving on this 15th century building represents on the one side a fox in a monk's hood preaching from a small pulpit to a congregation of geese, while on the other, the sermon finished, the fox is seen carrying off one of the geese in his mouth. The house, it is believed, was once the residence of Henry Tooley (whose tomb may be seen in St Mary Quay church). A few doors from this house was reputed to be the site of the cottage in which Gainsborough the famous artist lived while in Ipswich.' The buildings that can just be seen on the left in Lower Brook Street are where the *East Anglian Daily Times* and *Evening Star* offices are now.

Police drivers line up with their vehicles at the Great Gipping Street Drill Hall around 1958. These heavy, slow vehicles were the best available to the Ipswich County Borough Police in the fight against crime. The borough force was then based at the Town Hall. As vehicles came into greater use, the force used different locations in town to garage its transport. The first were kept in a small garage in George Street. A Humber Super Snipe was kept at the Golden Lion yard. Other sites included Lady Lane, West End Road and Woodbridge Road. The drivers include: PC George Bezant, PC Len Pugh, PC Raymond Giles and PC Victor Mayhew.

Station Street in the mid-1950s. Children are able to play in the relatively traffic-free street.

Harry Elliss ran his newsagent business from 58 St Matthews Street. He is seen standing at the
door with his wife Adelaide around 1912. The alleyway where the man leans against the wall
led to Garrett's Buildings, small houses which were demolished long ago. The sign over the door
dates the housing to 1867. The site of Elliss's shop was redeveloped in the late 1980s. BBC
Radio Suffolk now stands where Garrett's Buildings were.

This seventeenth-century building in St Matthews Street, the Golden Fleece Hotel, was
demolished in a 1960s redevelopment of the area. The shops that now stand on the site are set
further back, near BBC Radio Suffolk and close to Berners Street.

St Matthews Street in 1934. The open gateway led to F.W. Canham and Sons coach-building works. This picture was taken from St Matthews Church Lane, where Civic Drive is now. (Percy Chinery)

A picture of St Matthews Street taken at the same time as the one above. Just beyond the support pole for the trolleybus wires in the middle distance is the junction of Berners Street, with the curved frontage of Stead and Simpson's shoe shop on the far corner. The shops from the right include Hipps tailors, the Maypole dairy, Witherley's wool store, and the Royal bookshop. (Percy Chinery)

St Matthews Street from Westgate Street on 5 December 1966, with Smith's Albion House, 'Drapers and House Furnishers', on the corner of Lady Lane and, beyond, Bowhill Elliott's shoe shop. All of the buildings were replaced in the late 1960s.

The north side of St Matthews Street in 1963, with the Rainbow public house on the right of the picture.

St Matthews Street from Hyde Park Corner in 1964. Work to demolish the Rainbow public house (right) has begun. All of the buildings on the right were demolished in the redevelopment and widening of the street in the mid-1960s.

Majors Corner in the mid-1950s, showing the Bee Hive Inn which opened in 1899 and was demolished in 1960. This picture was taken from the front of the Regent Theatre. Upper Orwell Street is between the bus and the inn.

All of these old buildings in Foundation Street, photographed in the 1950s, have gone. The couple crossing the road are near the entrance to Wingfield Street. A multistorey car park now stands on the site.

Museum Street in the mid-1960s, with the Winter Trading Company, electrical wholesalers, premises on the left. Halfway along the left-hand side a lady is stepping out of the County Borough of Ipswich Treasurer's Office, where thousands queued to pay their rates. (Terry Neeves)

Princes Street on 10 February 1965. The roundabout at the junction with the new Civic Drive and Franciscan Way is being built. The British Lion public house was demolished in the redevelopment of the area. The glass-clad building of Willis Corroon now stands on this corner. The Greyfriars scheme and its block of flats is being constructed on the right of the picture.

Mason Street was a narrow road of terraced houses running from Victoria Street to Prospect Road which was lost in the redevelopment of the area in the late 1960s. This picture was taken on 4 January 1967, shortly before demolition.

CHAPTER TWO

THE DOCK & PORT

The Ipswich wet dock was completed in 1842, after the River Orwell had been redirected through the New Cut. The port now extends along the River Orwell on both banks. The next few pages give a glimpse of this important part of Ipswich in years past.

A Victorian view of the River Orwell from near the dock's lock gates. A promenade ran along New Cut through three lines of lime and poplar trees which were planted in 1846, and the area was a popular place for a walk. On the left of the picture is The Umbrella, a canopied shelter, with a statue of Pegasus next to it. In the distance is Hog Highland, where Cliff Quay is now. The promenade was lost to new railway sidings in the 1920s. (William Vick)

A view of the dock area from the air, taken in the mid-1930s. The huge works of Ransomes, Sims and Jefferies Ltd, agricultural and machinery manufacturers, dominate the foreground. The company was formed in 1789, when Robert Ransome started his foundry in the town. In the mid-1960s the works moved from this site to its present home at Nacton Road. The gasworks with its three gasometers is centre left. The Ipswich Gas Light Company was formed in 1821. The works were sighted at the dock to keep down the costs of coal imported for gas production. The houses of Albion Street, Albion Place, Bishop Street, Trinity Street, Unity Street and Wykes Bishop Street in the left corner are all gone. A ship is unloading cargo at Tovells Quay (centre right) while the masts of barges can be seen over the rooftops around the dock. On the far side of New Cut lies the engineering works of Ransomes and Rapier (top left), another of the town's major employers. 'R and R' was established in Ipswich in 1868 and covered over 14 acres. The Waterside Works employed thousands until its closure in September 1987. To the right of Ransomes and Rapier's site are the terraced houses of Bath Street, Purplett Street, Hartland Street, Bright Street, Tyler Street, Kemp Street, Felaw Street and Robinson Street, now mostly demolished.

A charming little group, complete with dog and puppies, on a barge at Flint Wharf in the late 1920s. (Titshall Brothers)

Hard graft for dock workers unloading a cargo of sulphate of lime. (Titshall Brothers)

Three barges at St Peters Dock near Stoke Bridge early in the twentieth century.

Thames barges tied up at Stoke Bridge in a view of around 1902. Barges would have carried seed to Mason's Mill (left) on St Peters Dock.

A sailing ship and barge tied up at the dock quay in the mid-1920s. The picture is taken from near Coprolite Street, looking towards the Custom House. The businesses were, from the left: Meux's Brewery Company Ltd, maltsters, the Pilot Inn (one of many public houses round the dock for the thirsty dock workers and seamen) and Thomas Mortimer Ltd, corn merchants and maltsters. (Bert Thrower)

Dockers take a break from work to pose for this picture at Cliff Quay in the late 1920s. In the centre background is one of the town's gasometers, which dominated the dock skyline. The top of Cliff Brewery is on the right. (Titshall Brothers)

Coal being discharged from the *Alice Marie* at Tovells Quay in 1934.

Thames barges moored on the River Orwell in December 1955, near the lock at the dock and looking towards where the West Bank terminal is today.

The barge *Venture* in the dock on 2 July 1956, taken from near the lock.

The tug *Stronghold* tows the clipper *Abraham Rhydburg* from the dock in the 1930s. In the background is Cliff Quay. The picture is taken from a magic lantern slide made by Billy Robinson, a member of the Ipswich and District Photographic Society.

CHAPTER THREE

THE WAR YEARS

Photographs of war damage are rare. Photography was very restricted in order that information about the accuracy of bombing raids might not be passed on to the enemy. The pictures in this section will give a small insight into life in the town during the Second World War. As the threat of war in Europe grew in the 1930s, measures were taken by companies to protect their staff from attack. In 1938 printers W.S. Cowell dug trenches and sandbagged them in the company cycle yard.

Staff of W.S. Cowell posing by the defences, with the buildings in Falcon Street in the background. The site is now part of the Buttermarket Shopping Centre. (W.C.S. Girling)

Ipswich suffered from bombing raids during the Second World War, its port and railway links being prime targets for the German Air Force. Inaccurate and indiscriminate bombing meant that residential areas were often hit, resulting in widespread death and terror. The first of fifty-two raids on Ipswich was on the night of 21 June 1940. Sirens sounded at 11.05 p.m. as bombs fell in the area. At 12.20 a.m. a Heinkel III flying at 18,000 ft dropped bombs over 700 yards of the northern part of the town; one hit a house in Dale Hall Lane (above). One of the rooms in the house had been converted to a shelter using sandbags. Mr and Mrs Robert and Stella Anderson and their maid, Miss Ruby Crawford, were killed. In the photograph, wardens are sorting through the wreckage of the house.

The front of the house in Dale Hall Lane, the first house in the town to be hit by a bomb.

The chimney stacks of the house in Dale Hall Lane were blown into the garden by the explosion.

This German bomber, a Dornier Do17, crashed and burned out in Gippeswyk Park at 6.26 p.m. on 21 August 1940. The crew had abandoned the aircraft after an attack by two Hurricanes of 56 Squadron over Claydon. The crew of four were captured, two injured and two unhurt.

This German bomber, a Dornier Do17 (the same as the one that crashed in Gippeswyk Park), was forced to crash-land at Spring Wood, Wickambrook, between Bury St Edmunds and Haverhill, after its port engine was hit by ground fire on 23 August 1940. It was *en route* for Coventry with its deadly load. The crew of four were captured unhurt. The aircraft was taken on a tour of the region for the public to inspect. The aircraft is seen in Christchurch Park with a crowd of fascinated onlookers gathered round.

Mrs and Miss Woodbine were trapped in their Anderson shelter at 'Windyridge', Woodbridge Road East, during an attack on 21 September 1940. A car was totally wrecked in the blast.

This fine old timber-framed building in Key Street had survived for hundreds of years, only to be destroyed by German bombing. The tower of the Custom House at the dock is in the top left corner of the picture.

A terrible disaster hit Cemetery Road in the early hours of 21 September 1940, when a mine landed in a stonemason's yard close by. The mine only partly exploded, wrecking a house and badly damaging twenty-five more, with blast damage to a further 150. A bomb disposal squad tried to make the mine safe, but a decision was taken to explode the mine where it lay at 8.00 p.m. on 23 September. The explosion that followed was far greater than expected. A crater 25 ft deep resulted, with seventy houses being destroyed and hundreds damaged. Windows hundreds of yards away from the blast were shattered.

Houses in Bloomfield Street were damaged in this German raid of 4 November 1940. The raid killed a boy at No. 132. The picture shows wardens in steel helmets working in the wreckage. Roofing timbers, furniture and the family bath lay tangled together.

In the same raid a woman was killed at 16 Fletcher Road. After dropping its bombs the Dornier's crew machine-gunned Foxhall Road.

Ten 50 kg bombs were dropped from a Dornier Do17 on Ipswich at 10.15 a.m. on 8 January 1941. At 6 Romney Road, where a baby was killed, wardens and neighbours are busy making the site safe.

The Felixstowe Road area came under attack on 24 March 1941. Nos 209 and 211 (opposite Murray Road) were hit. Five people were rescued from the debris by wardens and police.

Bomb damage close to the dock. The original caption to this picture reads, 'Bomb on East Anglian town. Another picture of the repair shop and store; no damage was done to the main buildings when a bomb fell on this plant in an East Anglian town on Tuesday.' Censors checked all pictures and captions before publication and specific location details were banned so as not to give the enemy accurate information about their bombing.

A bomb exploded at 29 Hamilton Road, killing six people, on 2 June 1942. At 5.25 a.m. a very low-flying aircraft firing cannon and machine guns dropped a 500 kg bomb, killing Mr and Mrs Cherry at No. 27, and Mr and Mrs Nunn and Miss Sillett at No. 29. The other victim died in hospital.

In the early hours of 2 June 1942 bombs rained from a German aircraft as it circled the town. Areas hit included houses at the corner of Shackleton Road and Badshah Avenue, Turner's Works in Foxhall Road, and houses in Dover Road, Exeter Road, Camden Road, York Road, Upper Cavendish Street, Kemball Street, Jefferies Road, St Helens Street, Palmerston Road, Wherstead Road and Bixley Road. In the picture Auxiliary Fire Servicemen take a tea break after firefighting at the corner of Badshah Avenue and Shackleton Road, where four houses and two bungalows were damaged. Bill Read (fourth right) recalls that the fire crew were on the scene at 2.00 a.m. and it took them all night to quell the flames.

Houses in Bixley Road damaged in the raid of 2 June 1942. Nos 123, 125, 127 and 129 were damaged by the blast.

At 125 Bixley Road four people had a remarkable escape. They were in a Morrison shelter, a steel cage used in the home as protection from the effects of the blast (in the centre of the picture). They were among ten people trapped in the rubble after the raid.

Tragedy struck Ipswich on the night of 25 August 1942, when a high-explosive bomb hit an Anderson shelter at 501 Nacton Road, killing a mother and her eight children. Three properties were seriously damaged.

A fireboat was sunk in one raid on the dock at Ipswich. The Custom House is in the right background.

Extensive damage in Myrtle Road on 2 June 1943. The original caption to this picture reads, 'When early morning raiders flew over an East Coast town on Wednesday morning ten people were killed and a number injured; one of the aircraft struck a crane (crashing near the lock gates) and was destroyed, with the occupants being killed. The picture shows a row of working-class houses which were struck by a high-explosive bomb; six houses were demolished and there were six fatal casualties.' War records show that there was a direct hit on a small general shop and houses; those killed included three people at No. 42, Mr and Mrs Martin and Mrs Sheppard, Mrs Mable Brown at No. 46, Mr and Mrs Smith at No. 44. A Mr Clows died later in hospital.

A V1 flying bomb damaged houses and killed four people when it landed in Halton Crescent at 11.25 p.m. on 18 October 1944.

Bomb-damaged buildings in Cliff Road. A gasometer at the gasworks at the corner of Holywells Road and Patterson Road is in the background.

Nine people were killed in Seymour Road, when high-explosive bombs fell on 4 March 1945. Six houses were demolished and six others seriously damaged in the attack.

Street parties were organized all over town when the war in Europe ended on 8 May 1945. Bunting was hung out in Withipoll Street for a children's Victory Tea on 19 May 1945. Victory over Japan came on 2 September, bringing to an end the Second World War.

Celebrations began all over town in May 1945. Residents of Parliament Road organized a street party, with bunting strung from the houses and tables down the middle of the road. Plates of cakes were baked for the special day. Eager young faces gather round for a picture in the early summer sunshine.
(H. Baxter)

CHAPTER FOUR

GETTING ABOUT

Trains, boats and planes are among the means of transport in this section. The railways brought long-distance travel to the masses in the Victorian era, but there was no organized transport across Ipswich until late in the last century. Railways, trams and other forms of transport changed life forever. People were able to work distances from their homes which had been impractical before. Ipswich was linked to London by rail in 1846. The town's horse-drawn trams came into service in 1880; these were replaced by the electric trams in 1903, which were in turn taken out of service in 1926. Trolleybuses took over the service until August 1963.

Pedal power provided a cheap means of transport, and in the early years of the twentieth century there were several cycling clubs in town. The club group are gathered outside the Safe Harbour Inn in Dorkin Street ready for an outing. Dorkin Street used to be where the Suffolk College is now.

A busy Cornhill in the 1890s. With all the flags and banners flying, the picture could well have been taken in 1897 during the celebrations for Queen Victoria's Diamond Jubilee. On the right, one of the town's horse-drawn trams stops for passengers; on the front of the tram is an advertisement for Fred Boon's cycle shop at 17 Crown Street. Buggy drivers weave their way through the crowds, as horse-drawn taxis line up with their bowler- and top-hatted drivers. On the extreme left, market traders are selling their goods in front of Mannings public house. Grimwade's shop, on the corner of Westgate Street, was extended to its present size to include the site of Trundles, the saddle and harness makers, in 1904. The banner hanging across the entrance to Westgate Street says, 'Men of England, be sober, be vigilant'.

Ipswich's electric tramway service started on 21 November 1903, replacing the horse-drawn service that had operated since October 1880, starting with a line between the railway station and the Cornhill. In February 1899 the Parliamentary Committee of the Ipswich Corporation had been endowed to negotiate the purchase of the tramways. The corporation purchased the tramways for £17,000, which was little more than half the money sunk in the enterprise by the shareholders. A power station was built in Constantine Road. The generating station, workshop and car shed were built by Mr S.A. Kenney of Ipswich, who was paid £26,984 for the generating station and £6,706 for the car shed. A refuse incinerator was also built on the site with a 178½ ft chimney, 4 ft higher than the Tower church spire. The laying of the tracks caused considerable disruption to the town, with lines running on all the main routes out of the centre. Over 10 miles of 3 ft 6 in gauge track were laid, several town centre buildings being demolished to make way for the new service through the narrow streets. The picture above shows Majors Corner from Carr Street, with St Helens Street running away from the camera, as tram rails are laid below street level. The Regent Theatre would be in the centre of this view today.

A double curve for the tram lines at the junction of Princes Street and Queen Street.

A group of children playing in St Helens Street, near the junction with Grove Lane, around 1906, as a tram trundles by.

Spring Road around 1908. One of the electric trams is in the centre and the railway viaduct in the background. The viaduct was constructed when the line from Westerfield to Felixstowe was built, opening in May 1877. At the time the Corporation complained that the Derby Road station was in the wrong place: it was three-quarters of a mile from the nearest built-up area of town.

A tram crosses busy Cornhill on a summer day around 1915. This postcard view from the front of the Town Hall includes the Picture House Cinema with its turret top in the centre of the photograph. The Picture House opened in 1912 and included a popular café. Boots the Chemists is on the site today.

An Ipswich Corporation tram outside the Station Hotel.

Derby Road from the railway bridge, around 1905, with the Railway Hotel in Foxhall Road in the background.

One of Ipswich's trams at the junction of Derby Road and Felixstowe Road, with the Royal Oak public house in the background. On the front of the tram is an advertisement for Poole's Picture Palace, a cinema in Tower Street which opened in 1909 in the old lecture hall. Admission in 1911 was 3d, 6d and 1s. The building later became the Arts Theatre.

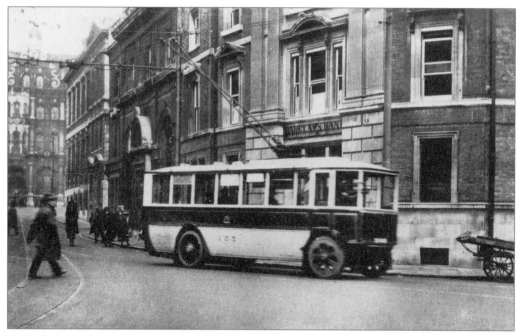

One of Ipswich's new 'trackless trams' turning from Princes Street into Queen Street in the 1920s. The trolleybuses started to replace the trams in 1923, with the closure of the tram system coming in July 1926.

St Matthews Street around 1930. A single-deck trolleybus, built by Garretts of Leiston, passes a splendid open-topped car outside the Ipswich Wireless Company, electrical engineers at No. 26a.

These Ipswich trolleybuses, photographed outside the Constantine Road depot, were built by Ipswich engineering company Ransomes, Sims and Jefferies in 1928; they were in service in the town until 1953. During the latter part of this period they were 'modernized' at the front.

An Eastern Counties open-topped bus at Nacton crossroads, on its way to Felixstowe in the 1920s.

An Ipswich Corporation trolleybus (No. 84) on the service from the Cornhill to Bourne Bridge. This bus was built by Ransomes, Sims and Jefferies in 1938 and was in service in the town until 1959. The Picture House Cinema in Tavern Street is in the background.

Trolleybus No. 113 in Crown Street in the early 1960s. (H.N. James)

Henri Salmet, the first airman to land at Ipswich, with his frail-looking Bleriot aircraft. His monoplane landed in a field near Stone Lodge Lane in August 1912. His tour of England was sponsored by the *Daily Mail*.

A pair of farm hands with their Dennis lorry, which has an unusual combination of solid wheels at the back and pneumatic tyres at the front. (Titshall Brothers)

The Oriental Café was at 21a Westgate Street. Its solid-tyred delivery van, with the café's phone number 430 on the side, was able to park *across* Crane Hill in London Road while this picture was taken in the 1920s. (Titshall Brothers)

A 1924-registered solid-tyred Thornycroft lorry belonging to Child and Pullin Ltd, haulage contractors, of 1a Portman Road, Ipswich. (Titshall Brothers)

This Chevrolet truck belonging to John Freston, hay, straw and corn dealers of Friars Bridge Road, Ipswich, was first registered in 1930. The proud pose of the driver and the gleam of the vehicle would suggest the picture was taken when the truck was new. (Titshall Brothers)

A Gilford lorry of the Danish Bacon Company Ltd of Denmark House, Foundation Street, Ipswich. (Titshall Brothers)

Freston's traded as haulage contractors from 36 Princes Street and Nos 15, 17 and 19 Tanners Lane. Their Chevrolet truck was first registered in Ipswich in 1928. (Titshall Brothers)

S. McNamara's garage at 111 St Helens Street in the mid-1920s. The sign on the wall proclaims: 'S. McNamara (late Daimler and Napier Co). Motor hoods trimming and painting. Specialities, one man hoods for touring cars and char-a-bancs, motor truck hoods, side screens.' The Model T Ford outside the neighbouring Phillips Bakery has a sign on the roof saying 'I Make Trickers Sausages'. (Titshall Brothers)

A 25 hp Daimler delivery lorry belonging to Tollemache Breweries with its draymen in Bath Street in the 1920s. This vehicle, with its solid tyres and gas lamps, was first registered by its original owners, the Unicorn Brewery, in 1919. (Titshall Brothers)

A line-up of cars taking those 'less fortunate' to Shrubland Park for an outing around 1915. This postcard view of the events has 'Cripples outing to Scrubland Park' printed on it with a misspelling of the day's destination.

An Ariel motorcycle, with cushions for the pillion passenger, was the choice of Leslie Piper of Paper Mill Lane, Bramford. (Titshall Brothers)

A pair of likely lads on their motorcycles in the 1920s. On the left is Bert Pryke, on a Carfield, with Bill 'Pally' Driver lined up beside him. Bert Pryke used to live at Paper Mill Farm, Bramford, and Bill Driver at Old Paper Mill Cottages, Bramford. The photograph comes from a time when turning your cap round to stop it blowing away was all the headgear a 'biker' needed. (Titshall Brothers)

This splendid 3½ hp Bradbury motorcycle was first registered in Ipswich on 16 June 1909 by Percy Leonard Smith of 38 Wherstead Road. Mr Smith ran a cycle and motorcycle shop from 1912 to 1927 at Nos 41, 43 and 45 Wherstead Road. Mr Smith's shop has advertisements in the window for cycles built with BSA and Eadie fittings; he was also agent for Veritas mantles for gas lamps.

CHAPTER FIVE

STEAM POWER

This chapter features rail locomotives, steam lorries, paddle-boats, road-rollers and farm machinery from the era before diesel engines.

A class AJ15 freight locomotive pulling into Ipswich station in 1937.

There was a rail disaster at Westerfield station on the morning of 25 September 1900 that cost two Great Eastern railwaymen their lives. The boiler of the locomotive of a goods train at the station exploded and the driver, 67-year-old John Barnard, was found scalded, badly injured and close to death 40 yards from his cab. He died within minutes. The body of fireman William Macdonald could not be found for some time. He was eventually found, dead, in the third truck of the train, his clothes in tatters. Also injured by the explosion was a policeman, PC Goodwin, who was trapped in a porter's hut, and a young boy who was close by.

Ipswich station around 1910, with three steam engines in view. In the centre of the picture, taken from the Ancaster Road Bridge, is a horse shunting a truck.

Baylham crossing on 25 October 1952. This fine old engine, built in the 1880s, is pulling the 3.55 p.m. from Bury St Edmunds to Ipswich. (H.N. James)

The Glasgow to Colchester through train, hauled by No. 61620 *Clumber*, passes under the old Great Eastern signal gantry near Gippeswyk Park in the early 1950s. (H.N. James)

Westerfield Junction around 1935, with B17 class No. 2806 *Audley End* at the platform. (H.N. James)

'Britannia' Pacific No. 70012 *John of Gaunt* enters Ipswich station from the tunnel on a London–Norwich service around 1955. (H.N. James)

Two young children watch from Gippeswyk Park as the Harwich to Peterborough train, hauled by No. 61646 *Gilwell Park*, pulls out of the station around 1952. (H.N. James)

Ipswich station in the mid-1950s, with B12 class locomotive No. 61533 at the platform.

A delivery of barrels by steam wagon to the Asylum Hotel, at the corner of Foxhall Road and Parliament Road, in 1907. The hotel changed its rather unattractive name in the 1920s. Now called Heathlands Hotel, it stands close to St Clements Hospital. In 1907 the hotel was open from six in the morning until ten in the evening and beer was 2d per pint. The steam wagon dray, made by Garretts of Leiston, was a slow workhorse, with carbide lamps and solid rubber tyres.

A road gang from Dawson and Company of Rushmere with their steamroller around 1910.

A steam wagon with solid tyres photographed by the Titshall Brothers on the outskirts of Ipswich during the 1920s. This clanking, puffing beast of the road must have been quite a sight as it made its way round.

New Cut in the 1920s, with the paddle steamer *Suffolk* tied up at the jetty. The Great Eastern Railway Company ran a service with three paddle steamers on the River Orwell to Felixstowe and Harwich from 1895 to 1930. The *Suffolk* was built by Earls of Hull in 1895, the *Essex* coming into service the following year. (Bert Thrower)

The *Norfolk*, which joined the service in 1900, sets sail from New Cut in the 1920s with a full load of passengers. (Bert Thrower)

A steam engine driving a threshing machine. A typical scene on the farm at harvest time captured by the Titshall Brothers.

Thick black smoke pours from the chimney of the traction engine driving the threshing machine in this view of a working farm in the period between the wars. In the right foreground is a water wagon that would be filled from the farm pond or stream to keep the steam engine running. (Titshall Brothers)

The two pictures on this page were taken at Belstead in the 1920s. This threshing scene includes Spencer Proctor, on the engine, Frank Southgate and Walter Grimwood. Walter began work with steam ploughs and threshing machines in 1872 and received a long-service award at the Suffolk Show in 1952, when aged 98, for sixty-five years' service. His son Harry received his award for forty-seven years' service on the same day. (Titshall Brothers)

A Burrell steam engine at the rear of the Belstead smithy in the 1920s. In the picture are (left to right): Harry Grimwood, Walter Grimwood and George Ward. (Titshall Brothers)

CHAPTER SIX

OUT OF TOWN

*This chapter shows a little of life outside the town in the days when horses still helped work the
land and visits to Ipswich were special occasions.*

Most small communities had a blacksmith like this one photographed by the Titshall Brothers.

Children walk down Chapel Lane, Great Blakenham, early in the twentieth century.

Alnesbourne Priory Farm, on the banks of the River Orwell at Nacton, in the early years of the twentieth century. The founders of the priory that once stood on the site are not known. The priory was dedicated to the Blessed Virgin Mary. Three churches once stood on the land of the priory – Hallowtree, St Petronnell and Bixley. Margaret Catchpole's father worked here as a farm labourer. In recent years the 'Priory' has been a nightclub and a holiday centre.

A postcard view of Nacton post office around 1905.

A very smart William Keeble, who delivered milk for Orwell Park Dairies at Nacton, pictured with his cart and gleaming churns at Post Office Hill in the late 1920s. (Titshall Brothers)

A Great Eastern Railway bus outside the Red Lion Inn at Chelmondiston.

A Great Eastern Railway service bus outside the Bristol Arms at Shotley. The registration number is F 1614. This bus was one of twelve built in 1905 at the railway company's Stratford Works, costing around £600 each. The service to Shotley commenced in 1905, running until August 1916. It restarted in 1919 and was sold to its competitor, Eastern Counties Road Car Company Ltd, which later amalgamated with Eastern Counties.

As the Titshall Brothers toured the area with their mahogany and brass stand camera in the 1920s and '30s, they captured some fine characters. This couple outside their flint cottage have brought their splendid wind-up record player into the garden for the picture; this piece of equipment was, no doubt, their pride and joy.

Ploughing with a pair of horses near Ipswich around 1925. (Titshall Brothers)

A team of three horses pulls a harrow weighed down with logs across a field near Ipswich. (Titshall Brothers)

A well-known character in Sproughton was Bob Jacob, known as 'Sproughton Bob'. His home was a thatched cottage in the High Street. He never attended school and was illiterate, and when his home burnt down he lived rough. He did odd jobs in the area, sorting pea sticks and wood for making broaches for thatching. Farmers employed him to scare rooks from the crops. Bob had a good knowledge of wildlife. When he died in the 1920s a collection was made for a wreath for him.

This fine old Suffolk character was 'Clinker' Clarke. He is photographed here with his daughter and granddaughter outside their tiny home at Grundisburgh Corner around 1928. The harsh life style of the period is ingrained on the faces of these country folk. (Titshall Brothers)

A group of young children outside Mill Cottage, Grundisburgh, in 1929. The cottage had a hand-operated water pump in the garden.

A pair of Model T Ford charabancs set off from the Half Moon at Grundisburgh around 1926, on an outing to Great Yarmouth. The vehicles for this adventure were provided by Canhams of Woodbridge. (Titshall Brothers)

The group from the Half Moon at Grundisburgh line up for the camera. Providing the music for a singsong after a few pints of Cobbold's brew was Bill Bennett with his accordion. (Titshall Brothers)

The High Street, Needham Market, around 1905. Younger children pose for the camera as a lad prepares to pull down a blind on the front of the building on the right. In the centre of the picture is the King's Head public house.

Children in Capel St Mary Street around 1906.

Coddenham post office in the 1920s. A postman with a full bag of mail appears about to set off on his motorcycle and sidecar (registration BJ4732). One sign by the door reads 'Postal Telegraph Office', the other 'Money Order Office, Post Office and Savings Bank'. (Titshall Brothers)

ACKNOWLEDGEMENTS

My thanks to those who have contributed to my collection of photographs and to those who have passed on valuable caption information and helped make this book possible.

Gordon Kinsey • Doug Cotton • Ron Havel • H. Baxter • Ralph Chinery
John Hawkins • Christine Hubert • Mr and Mrs E. Thrower
Mr and Mrs W.C.S. Girling • Andy Calvesbert • Neville Smith
Dr John Blatchly • Bill Nash • Terry Neeves • Iris Howard • H.N. James
Brian Brownlee-Pinkerton • Colin Barber • Derrick Neave • Edward Storey
Brenda Orris • Veronica Overall • Bob Clow • Cecelia Davey • Anne King
Monica Little

PART TWO

IPSWICH REVISITED

A girl in the garden of her home in Ipswich, *c.* 1920. The photograph captures the fashion for clothes and toys perfectly. Her coat and hat are a copy of adults' of the period, as are her doll's pram and clothes.

INTRODUCTION

Welcome to *Ipswich Revisited*, a fascinating look at Ipswich from years ago. For many, memories will come flooding back as they look at the town and events of yesteryear, with pictures not only of the town and its streets, but also of its people; the way they worked, lived and played.

Ipswich is a town where folk have deep roots. Generations of the same families have always lived locally. You can find a common acquaintance in a room of half a dozen strangers at any gathering in town; it's just one big village, and everybody knows somebody their friends and relatives know. This gives a sense of belonging, and leads to a great interest in local history, unlike many other towns, packed with commuters who do not even know their neighbours.

Photography has provided a marvellous medium to record detail; everybody finds some different point of interest in any photograph. A simple street scene will catch the eye of some who are interested in vintage transport, while others will be reminded of their favourite shops or public house, while many find the clothes of passers-by fascinating.

As soon as photography was invented in the late 1830s it naturally became the perfect means to record life. There is a Hollywood myth of the past, perfectly tailored clothes, pristine cars and machines, and well-fed faces. But the study of old photographs soon dispels this image: life was very often harsh, and no amount of re-creation captures the mood. Sadly, much is not recorded on film. Old, often shabby, housing is swept away without being photographed, and all that remains are a few memories, soon lost forever as the generations pass. There is much of the town from the past that I have never seen – the housing around Rope Walk and The Mount, for example. Unless commissioned, professional photographers do not generally record street scenes, and even though most people now have access to a camera, how many of them take pictures of a town's streets today? What was often rather mundane when old pictures were taken becomes the point of interest years later. A row of shops is not the greatest challenge to a photographer, and parked cars were usually in the way at the time, but now the vehicles and shops are of intense interest with the passing of the years. Often in Edwardian postcard scenes there is a group of children in the foreground. Perhaps the photographer would have preferred them out of the way, but now, a century later, those children bring the picture to life.

The end of the Second World War in 1945 was cause for great celebration. Although the war continued in the Far East, VE-Day saw many street parties in Ipswich. I have featured several pictures from that period of joy. Many pictures would have been taken on simple box cameras, but they are no less important than the pictures taken by Reg Fisk of Tudor Photos, who toured the town and took many pictures of the street parties.

I have devoted a large number of pictures to the 1950s, a time of great change in the town; many who were around then will enjoy the memories of those years. Some wonderful images capture the decade perfectly.

Thousands will recall the heyday of speedway racing at Foxhall Stadium, when the 'Witches' were formed in the early fifties. People flocked to the track at the edge of town when exciting live entertainment was much needed after the difficult times of the war years. Many locals can still recall names such as Sid Clarke, 'Titch' Read and Bert Edwards from the speedway era. I have included several pictures from the camera of Don Harris at Foxhall Stadium; he was a regular in the pits and on the first bend with his quarter-plate camera.

I am often asked where all the photographs in my collection have come from. There is a simple answer. Often, old collections of unidentified, unprinted negatives turn up. I am always interested in exploring these, and as a professional photographer I have the knowledge and the facilities to bring out the best in the pictures. I did not set out to become a collector of photographs, but simply decided to collect a few examples of Victorian techniques, having seen a daguerreotype belonging to a friend and photographic colleague, Terry Neeves. One glass negative led to a few more, and now I have many images that I am convinced would have been otherwise thrown away for want of a home. I am able to share them through the pages of the *Evening Star*, of which I am the picture editor, and this series of books. Each time, I have thought 'this is the last book', but often a phone call will lead to someone who has more negatives in need of care.

The postcard photographers who sold pictures of events, disasters and local street scenes provided a rich vein of pictures. No photographers work in this way now, selling pictures, often door to door, of small events and street scenes, so this type of record simply does not exist now. I have copied picture postcards in ones and twos and over the years they have built up into a comprehensive set of once scattered images. I have made every effort to date the photographs accurately, and I trust that the information on the back of the prints is largely correct. You reach the point where you can check no more, so forgive me if you know better! I hope you enjoy this book.

David Kindred

A party in Beck Street to celebrate the Coronation of Queen Elizabeth II in June 1953.

CHAPTER SEVEN

AROUND THE TOWN

Staff and customers of Walter Carter's bakery at the corner of Brooks Hall Road and Norwich Road pose for the camera, c. 1900.

Bramford Road at the junction of Prospect Road (right), *c.* 1912.

Another view of Bramford Road, this one at the corner of Bulwer Road, *c.* 1912. This photo features a charming group of children watching the photographer at work. The shop on the corner is W. and E. Denny's pork butchers shop offering 'Dairy fed pork' and 'Home made Sausages'.

Ransomes, Sims & Jefferies is an Ipswich company world famous for its grass-cutting equipment. One of their local customers in the 1890s was the gardener at Rushmere Villa. This print from an original glass negative is titled simply 'Albert and mowing machine'.

Robinson's newsagents at the corner of Back Hamlet and Grove Lane, *c.* 1915. The business moved to 137 Foxhall Road in about 1930.

The main buildings shown here in Bridge Street, including the Crown public house (centre) have all been demolished and the site is now part of the Stoke Bridge traffic system. The same view today would feature the Novotel hotel.

An enterprising service in the 1930s was this mobile Home Services Library from Copdock, offering a selection of humour, romance, and mystery titles.

A delivery boy from Brewer's grocery stores, St Matthews Street, pauses for the camera of keen photographer Percy Chinery, near his home in London Road. Mr Chinery also took the top picture. The allotments shown in the background of both pictures are still there today.

This postcard view from around 1910 is titled 'Majors Corner'. It features Bond Street, the Mitre Tavern (left) on the corner of St Helens Street, and Majors Corner in the middle distance. The man on the ladder is working on the County Hall building.

Another postcard view, this one shows St Helens Street looking towards Majors Corner, with the County Hall in the centre, c. 1918. On the extreme right is the Great Eastern Railways receiving office with Lancelot Ashford's piano tuning business beyond at no. 53.

A postcard view of St Helens Street and the corner of Regent Street (left), *c.* 1907. The spire of St Helens Church is visible at top right.

The Belvedere public house in Cox Lane in the late 1920s. This part of the town housed a thriving community in its tiny streets, now all cleared to make way for a car park. The pub was rebuilt as the General Gordon and is now the Earl Roberts.

The wedding of Florence Clarke and Frank Townsend at St Bartholomew's Church, 17 February 1928. This charming group captures the fashions of the era perfectly.

Staff from the self-raising department at Cranfield Brothers Ltd, flour millers, of St Peters Street, in the 1920s.

A rather serious group of girls at St Margarets School in 1928. Most of the girls are wearing smock tops to keep their clothes clean. It was still the norm for photographers taking group pictures to include a slate with the group's identity chalked on it; this one simply says 'St Margarets Group II'.

Ranelagh Road from near the junction with Ancaster Road (right), *c.* 1915. Almost all the houses on the left have been demolished.

Fore Street, *c.* 1910. At this time, the street was full of shops serving the local community, most of whom lived in terraced housing in the dock area. On the left at nos 90–92 is C.B. Gyford's fruiterers and greengrocers. The lady is looking in the window of Edward Haggar's butchers shop, next door to the Old Neptune Inn.

F.W. Woolworth's store in Carr Street in the 1920s. All of the buildings on the right, including the Lyceum Theatre and the offices and printing works of the *East Anglian Daily Times* and *Evening Star* have since been replaced by the Eastgate shopping centre.

This is the reverse view to the picture above and shows Carr Street with the Lyceum Theatre in the foreground. The theatre was built in 1890–1 at a cost of £9,000, but closed in 1936.

An Edwardian view showing the junction of Felixstowe Road and Bishops Hill. On the left is a drinking trough for horses.

Felixstowe Road, with Alston Road leading off to the right, *c.* 1910.

Herbert Wells' butchers shop in Fore Street (opposite the swimming baths) attracted huge queues in the 1940s for his sausages. Also shown are F.J. Southgate, hairdresser, and Smyth Brothers, ironmongers.

Lord Haldane inspecting some immaculately turned out nurses during his visit to the town on 13 May 1911.

Here the guard of honour stands to attention as Lord Haldane steps into his car after opening the new drill hall in Great Gipping Street.

Lord Kitchener also visited Ipswich, where he attended a scout rally at Portman Road sports ground (where the football club is today). Here Kitchener, wearing a blue serge suit and bowler hat, is inspecting the scouts. Reports said 'photographers were firing at his Lordship without intermission, but he seemed unconcerned'.

The scouts enjoyed an open air tea party after Lord Kitchener's visit.

Cliff Quay now stands where children played in the 1920s. On the right is the huge gasometer at the gas works near the wet dock. Work to enlarge the port began in 1923, extending along land known as Hogg Highland, a popular tree-lined area. Steam-powered piling equipment can be seen in the centre.

A postcard view from the gasometer, overlooking the lock gates, 1920s. In the centre and now replaced by the West Bank terminal, is Stoke bathing place, an open air swimming pool that was little more than a walled off area of the River Orwell with changing huts.

Lloyds Avenue from Tower Ramparts, early 1930s. The arch through the Lloyds building on the Cornhill was cut during 1929 and opened to traffic on 5 January 1930.

A postcard view of Tavern Street, looking towards the junction of Dial Lane and Tower Street, c. 1915.

Staff pose outside
George Bernard's
coffee house at
42 St Margarets
Street. Next door is
the premises of
John Spencer,
chimney cleaner.

Northgate School photographed from the air soon after it opened in the 1930s.

Bixley Road, part of the new by-pass, in the 1930s. This view from near the junction with Felixstowe Road shows an almost traffic-free road.

A huge fire completely destroyed the premises of R.D. & J.B. Fraser in April 1912. Built in 1890 at the corner of Museum Street and Princes Street, the store was rebuilt after the fire and today houses an insurance office.

Another huge blaze in Ipswich wrecked E.R. & F. Turner Limited's engineering works in Quadling Street early in the twentieth century. Postcard photographers were quick to feed the public's fascination with disaster at a time when local newspapers did not yet include photographs with their reports.

Church bell-founder Alfred Bowell had premises in Wykes Bishop Street, which used to run from Fore Hamlet to near the dock. This picture shows members of his staff with bells for Ditchingham Church, Norfolk, in 1931.

Staff at Alfred Bowell's pose with bells for Kirby-le-Soken Church, Essex.

Argyle Street from St Helens Street, *c.* 1908. The school building on the left is now part of University College, Suffolk. Many of the houses on the right were demolished in the 1950s.

Burlington Road from Barrack Corner, *c.* 1905.

Crowds filled the Cornhill in September 1905 to see General William Booth, the founder of the Salvation Army.

The proclamation of King George V, who succeeded to the throne in 1910, was another event that had crowds thronging the Cornhill.

This postcard view from Wherstead Road shows the junction of Vernon Street and Austin Street (left), *c*. 1915. The public house on the left, Uncle Tom's Cabin (now the Orwell Mariner) was a popular ale house for the residents of the hundreds of terraced houses in the area. All of the buildings except the pub

have now gone, including the fine house and horse drinking trough on the right. Once again, notice the almost traffic-free streets.

Flags flying on the Duke of Sussex public house in Cumberland Street to celebrate the Coronation of King George VI on 12 May 1937.

A policeman on point duty, directing traffic at the busy junction of Tavern Street and Carr Street, *c*. 1905. The White Horse Hotel's frontage has been altered in recent years and now includes shops.

The Prince of Wales, later (briefly) King Edward VIII, flew in from Northolt to perform the official opening of Ipswich's airport. Later that day he visited Ransomes, Sims & Jefferies' Orwell Works in Duke Street. This photograph was taken as he travelled down Bishops Hill, near the junction with Myrtle Road, where the 'Long Live the Prince' sign is. Almost everything in this picture has been demolished.

The world famous Barnum and Bailey circus came to Ipswich in 1898 and 1899, attracting huge crowds to the town. Based at a site near Bramford Road, the circus animals were paraded through the town. These four photographs were taken as they came down Fonnereau Road.

Here, teams of zebra pull floats featuring nursery rhyme characters.

The huge team of circus horses about to turn on to St Margarets Plain.

Armoured knights paraded on horseback in 1898. The buildings on the right have now been replaced by the Bethesda Baptist Church.

The Wolsey Pageant was held in Christchurch Park during the 1930s. These ladies pose on the steps of a special set built in front of Christchurch Mansion.

Spring Road with Bartholomew Street off to the right, c. 1912.

These buildings at the corner of St Margarets Street (right) and Soane Street were altered during the widening of St Margarets Street in the early 1930s. The right half was rebuilt with the gable ends 'turned' to face St Margarets Street (*see* below).

St Margarets Plain, 1950. On the right is the building featured in the top picture. The Running Buck public house is on the left.

A Christmas card showing the Ancient House bookshop, 1908.

This new building in Tacket Street was photographed in the mid-1930s. G.W. Hales, dispensing chemist, and photographic specialist, was then the main occupier of the building.

The passengers of a horse and buggy pose outside the premises of Charles Ingham, Beer Retailer, at nos 76 and 78 Woodbridge Road, near Argyle Street.

W. Webster, photographer of The Studio Royal, 105 St Helens Street, took this picture outside his premises (right) in the mid-1890s. The site is now part of Wells Court flats.

Fore Hamlet from the bottom of Bishops Hill, late 1940s. The van is just passing the entrance to Cavendish Street, off to the right.

An Edwardian view of Finchley Road. In those days it was lit with gas lamps.

Ipswich.   Meet of the Hounds in Constable Road, 1902.

A meet of the hounds in Constable Road, 1902.

The Old Manor House on St Margarets Green still stands today although the ivy and the iron railings shown here have disappeared.

In medieval times the Cornhill, or Market Hill as it was also known, was the town's principal trading centre. The earliest known plan of Ipswich, drawn in 1610, shows how the main roads through the town converged at this point. Throughout the history of the borough it has been a meeting place for large gatherings and markets. The post office building on the right replaced the Corn Exchange in 1881. This picture was taken in the 1920s looking towards Tavern Street from the window of Grimwades shop. Two single-decker trolley buses, which came into service in the mid-1920s to replace the trams, are featured in the foreground.

A postcard view of the Town Hall (right) and post office, *c.* 1912. The line of taxis is an interesting mixture of motor cars and horse-drawn cabs. The cab ranks moved to Lloyds Avenue when it opened in 1930.

The Cornhill, looking into Westgate Street in the early 1930s. This is the reverse view of the Cornhill from the picture shown opposite. The Lloyds Avenue arch, which opened in 1930, and Footman's Waterloo House store (now Debenhams) are on the right.

Derby Road railway station, *c.* 1890. The line from Ipswich to Felixstowe opened in May 1877.

Tacket Street Congregational Church, 1930. The demolition of shops on the corner of Cox Lane gave a much better view of the church. The twin spires have since been removed and the church renamed Christchurch. The pawnbrokers' sign (top right) belonged to Bradbrook's clothiers shop at 1 Orwell Place; they also offered a pawnbroking service.

A cargo of sugar being unloaded at Flint Wharf in the wet dock, 1920s. The sugar was for Burton, Son & Sanders Ltd, wholesale grocers and provision merchants, of College Street.

A 1920s promotional card for Frederick Sennitt's provision store at 18 Carr Street.

A huge blaze destroyed parts of R. & W. Paul's site at Ipswich dock on 24 January 1910. This picture 'taken at midnight' by Tunn and Company was one of a series of postcards of the disaster on sale to the public.

This fine pair of horse and carts belonged to Walter Pipe and Company of Derby Road, who offered the 'Finest House Coals'. The numbers on the front of the horses would seem to suggest that they were taking part in a competition.

CHAPTER EIGHT

TRANSPORT

This section of the book looks at various forms of transport, many of which influenced the town's development. Ipswich's origins lie in the River Orwell, the port and the crossing point at Stoke Bridge, while the construction of the wet dock, which opened in 1842, brought extra trade to the heart of the town. The railway from London was completed in June 1846, making travel easier for the masses. This splendid sailing ship, the Arthur Fitger, is pictured in the wet dock on 18 April 1900.

The Great Eastern Railway Company ran a paddle-steamer service from the New Cut (shown here), Ipswich to Harwich and Felixstowe between 1895 and 1930. The trees in the background were part of a popular promenade lost through commercial development of the island site during the 1920s.

Two young ladies with their cycles at Rushmere in 1900. Their style of dress must have made cycling difficult.

The charabanc, a mixture of open-topped bus and car, was a popular means of transport for days out. Public houses often arranged trips to the coast or visits to country pubs for darts competitions and so on. No doubt loaded with a few beers, this group is leaving the Vernon Arms in Whip Street, sometime in the 1920s.

Another outing from the Vernon Arms. Unlike the charabanc in the top picture, this one did not have the new pneumatic tyres to smooth the ride.

Electric trams came into service in 1903, replacing the horse-drawn vehicle service. They ran on main routes to the edge of town until they were in turn replaced in the 1920s by the trolley bus or 'trackless trams'. The last electric tram service ran in July 1926.

An electric tram on Bishops Hill, at the junction with Myrtle Road (right), *c.* 1905.

A row of double-decker trolley buses outside the Royal Showground at Chantry in 1934. A special service was arranged to transport the thousands of visitors to the Show from the town centre. The Showground now lies under the Chantry housing estate. All these buses were built by Ransomes, Sims & Jefferies in 1933 and 1934.

A single-decker trolley bus, built by Ransomes, Sims & Jefferies, in Adair Road in 1926. This unit was withdrawn from service in 1950 and used as a store at Pakefield near Lowestoft, and was later acquired by Ipswich Transport Society for preservation.

This trolley bus overturned on Bishops Hill on 8 June 1955.

Another accident – trolley bus 123 collided with the Crown public house in Bridge Street, sometime in the 1950s.

Trolley bus 64, built by Ransomes, Sims & Jefferies in 1936, on the Cornhill. This 48-seater was withdrawn from service in 1951. Originally sold to a dealer of Church Lane, Sproughton, it was bought in 1952 by a fruit merchant who used it as a shed at his premises in Sproughton Road. It was finally broken up on 5 November 1964.

Crown Street, early 1960s. Trolley bus 107 turns from Tower Rampart bus station on to Crown Street, passing Egertons garage. The garage site is now occupied by Crown Pools.

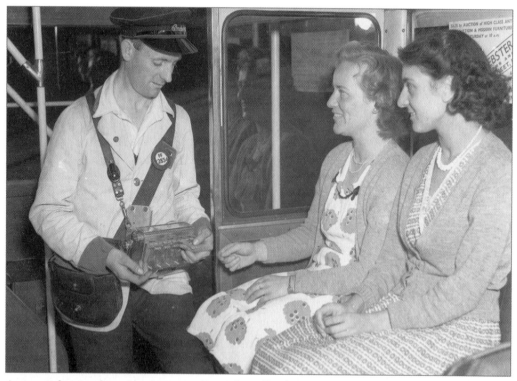

A new ticket machine in use on an Ipswich trolley bus, 30 August 1951. Trolley buses were taken out of service in August 1963.

Horse-drawn taxi cabs lined up outside the post office on the Cornhill, 16 March 1900.

Taxi cabs outside the post office, *c.* 1910.

The great days of steam trains are recalled by these two pictures. At Ipswich station in 1931 is a class B17/2 locomotive, number 2810, *Honningham Hall* of the London & North Eastern Railway Company. The train was the express for Cambridge, and the first coach was a six-wheel Great Eastern clerestory dating from the turn of the twentieth century.

A class D15, no. 8880, piloting an unidentified class B17 at the station, also in 1931.

CHAPTER NINE

SPORT & LEISURE

In this section we will look at some of the sport and leisure activities that local folk have enjoyed during the last century. The first pictures include some remarkable photographs taken of amateur sports in and around Rushmere at the turn of the twentieth century. We also look at early tennis fashion, speedway in its heyday in the 1950s, cricket and football. This photograph shows the ladies' cricket teams from Rushmere and Falkenham in the late 1890s.

This charming sports scene from the 1890s shows the Rushmere ladies' cricket team posed for the camera seated on a farm wagon. Their formal dress (by today's standards) must have made it very difficult for them to run and field. Almost everybody is wearing a hat for the event. The picture helps break down the myth that Victorians were all stern-faced – by this time photography was 'instantaneous', removing the need to sit perfectly still for several seconds which made it so difficult to hold a smile.

Another picture from the Rushmere vs Falkenham ladies' cricket match, with a fine selection of fashions from the period.

Rushmere vs Playford. It is difficult to believe the lady holding the bat could stay long at the wicket dressed as she is; although the bowler probably could not even see the wicket, cries of 'skirt before wicket' would have sounded a little odd!

Gentlemen modelling their tennis outfits at Rushmere in the late 1890s.

A fine pair at the wicket at Rushmere in the 1890s.

Hardly the 'leggy' look of modern tennis for these elegant young ladies at Rushmere in the 1890s.

It is not clear whether this picture was taken as a joke. The rather stern faces suggest not, but exactly why the Ipswich Tramways football team should be wearing top hats for their team photograph in 1906 we might never know. The Tramways service would have had a large staff of both drivers and conductors from which to select their teams. At the Constantine Road depot there was a large maintenance crew, and the town's first power station and waste disposal incinerator was run by the Tramways service. The power station was built to provide a service for the electric trams, although electricity was also supplied to domestic and commercial users. It was replaced by Cliff Quay power station in the 1950s. The town's refuse was also disposed of in an incinerator at the site. The 178½ ft chimney that served the site was demolished in the 1950s but the other buildings are still standing, and part still functions as the main depot and offices for Ipswich Buses Ltd.

A more conventional Ipswich Tramways team.

Gainsborough Athletic football club team, season 1932/33.

The Orwell Works athletic club team of Ransomes, Sims & Jefferies with their trophies, *c.* 1912.

Ipswich Town football club team, season 1906/07.

Many happy hours were spent on the *River Lady* which took pleasure trippers on the River Orwell from New Cut to Harwich Harbour, on the same route taken years earlier by the paddle-steamers of the Great Eastern Railway. This picture was taken on 24 May 1956 as the vessel neared Bourne Bridge. In the background are the three distinctive chimneys of Cliff Quay power station.

The Ipswich Sports at the Portman Road sports ground in 1912 included a tug-o'-war event.

A family Christmas before the age of television. In those days everybody gathered for the day to enjoy traditional games. The pictures on these two pages were taken by keen amateur photographer 'Charlie' Girling of Powling Road. Mr Girling recorded events in the town spanning seven decades. This picture from the 1930s shows his family and friends gathered for a typical Christmas tea with chicken, celery, pickles, jelly, and mince pies. Paper hats from the Christmas crackers are another feature of the picture. Mr Girling's final picture project was the construction of the Buttermarket shopping centre, which he photographed when he was in his eighties!

A festive game of snooker. Photographer Mr Girling is on the left.

Playing bagatelle. A present for one of the children, the game was evidently enjoyed by all.

Speedway racing came to Ipswich when Foxhall Stadium was built in 1950. Every Thursday night throughout the early and mid-1950s, crowds of up to twenty thousand people would make their way to the stadium to cheer on 'The Witches'. Spectators either walked, cycled, or took special buses to the stadium at this time since relatively few had motor transport of their own to reach the track. Pictured here at a practice session are John Laurie (left), Bob Sharpe (centre), and Dennis Day.

'The Witches' team, 1956. On the bike is team captain Bert Edwards and standing behind him, from left to right, are 'Junior' Bainbridge, Len Silver, Bill Bryden, Bob Sharpe, Ken Last and 'Titch' Read.

A capacity crowd at the stadium in April 1953. Here, from left to right, Johnnie Chamberlain, Harold NcNaughton, and 'Titch' Read break from the start.

'Witches' Bert Edwards (left) and 'Junior' Bainbridge on the concrete start grid.

First bend action from the 1950s with Dennis Day (left) and Sid Clarke in the lead.

Managers and team members handing out the food and drink at the 'Witches' supporters club Christmas party.

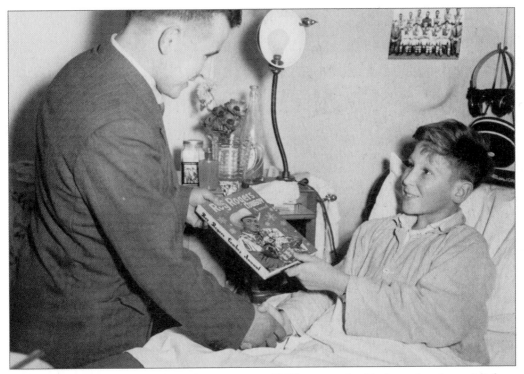

This young patient in hospital at Christmas time 1955 was no doubt cheered up by a visit from speedway rider 'Titch' Read who presented him with a copy of the Roy Rogers Christmas Annual.

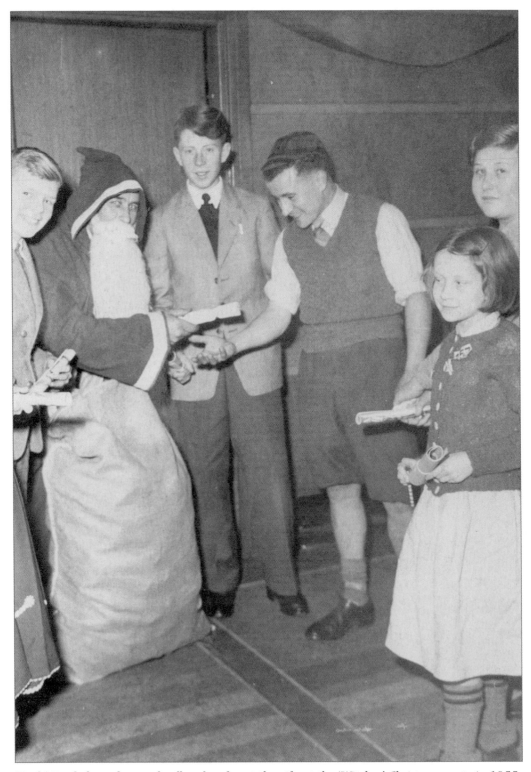

'Titch' Read, dressed as a schoolboy, hands out the gifts at the 'Witches' Christmas party in 1955.

The Ipswich speedway team, 1957. Back row, left to right: Otto Holubeck, Bob Sharpe, Cyril Roger, Peter Moore, Danny Dunton. Front row: Len Silver, Bert Edwards, 'Junior' Bainbridge.

The Ipswich team lined up on the centre green in front of another huge crowd, 25 April 1953.

Almost every fête, fun day and sports event featured a Peters ice-cream seller. This popular Ipswich-made ice-cream holds fond memories for generations of Ipswich children. A horse-drawn wagon was one sales point, photographed here on St Margarets Green by Percy Chinery in 1933.

A hand cart of Peters ice-cream in London Road in the 1930s.

CHAPTER TEN

VICTORY CELEBRATIONS

The grim years of the Second World War came to an end in May 1945. Although the war continued in the Far East it was time to celebrate victory in Europe. Street parties were held all over Ipswich. The next few pictures show hundreds of smiling faces celebrating the good news. This photograph is another from the camera of 'Charlie' Girling, who is actually in the picture holding the clacker alarm. It was taken at Cowell's printing works and shows the air raid wardens who worked through the war years to help defend the town.

Lancing Avenue.

Long Street.

Bramford Lane.

Grange Road.

Gatacre Road.

Brunswick Road.

More smiles in Brunswick Road.

Thousands attended the VE-Day celebrations on Tower Ramparts car park (now the bus station). Bands played and children danced. In the background is Tower Ramparts School, now the site of the shopping centre.

Golf Hotel, Foxhall Road.

Sidegate Lane.

Waterworks Street.

Phoenix Road.

Leighton Road.

More celebrations on the Gainsborough estate.

Brookfield Road.

Beech Grove.

CHAPTER ELEVEN

THE FIFTIES & SIXTIES

As with so many towns, the fifties and sixties saw huge changes in Ipswich. Old housing in the town centre was cleared to make way for road schemes and commercial development, and the population moved into housing estates like Chantry and Maidenhall. Fortunately the largely Victorian Cornhill buildings survived. In this section we will see some of those changes in progress and also capture some of the flavour of life in the town in this period of change. This picture, taken from the Lloyds building in 1951, shows cars parked in front of the Town Hall and queues for buses on what is now a pedestrianized area.

Lloyds Avenue, 3 April 1956. Footmans store is on the left.

Princes Street covered in a tangle of trolley bus wires. This picture is undated but it was probably taken on the same day as the one above.

The Cornhill from the first-floor window of the Golden Lion Hotel in 1951. A policeman on point duty is controlling traffic at the entrance to Lloyds Avenue, and cars park freely around the town centre.

Another view of the Cornhill in 1951.

The Cornhill, looking towards Westgate Street, *c.* 1960.

A postcard view of the Cornhill from near the Town Hall in the early 1960s.

The horse drinking trough on the corner of Portman Road and Princes Street was dismantled
and removed on 17 January 1961.

The Hippodrome Theatre in St Peters Street opened on 28 March 1905 and offered music hall and pantomime shows. Film shows started in 1930. The building closed as a theatre in 1957. It became the Savoy ballroom and a bingo hall before demolition in 1985.

Australian acrobat Eddie Ash performing an amazing stunt on the roof of the Hippodrome in the mid-1950s.

Two photographs of the conversion of the Hippodrome in June 1959. The seats had to be lifted to make way for the dance floor, and the piano was removed from the stage.

The Cobbold family's mansion in Holywells Park was built in 1814. Lord Woodbridge purchased the park and mansion in the 1920s and presented them to the town. In its latter years the mansion served as a community centre and youth club but it fell into disrepair and was demolished in 1962. The stable block and clock tower are still there but there are now gardens on the site of the mansion. This photograph was taken on 13 April 1959.

During the 1950s an otter caused considerable damage to the pond life in Holywells Park. It was eventually caught by hounds. Here the hunters proudly show off their catch in front of the mansion.

A market trader in London Road shows the crowd a fine pair of stockings during the 1950s.

Bananas on sale in the market in the 1950s.

A parade of elephants from Chipperfields circus makes its ponderous way along Ranelagh Road from the station on 27 March 1955. Visiting circuses used a site at the corner of Ranelagh Road and London Road.

Elephants from Chipperfields circus in Princes Street on 3 October 1961.

The car park at Tower Ramparts, 3 August 1956. This is now the Tower Ramparts bus station. The large building on the left was Tower Ramparts School. In the centre is Electric House, the showrooms and offices of Eastern Electricity. Egerton's garage in Crown Street is on the right.

The Beehive Inn at the corner of Upper Orwell Street (left) and Carr Street opened in 1899. This view from near the Regent Theatre (then the Gaumont), was taken on 23 March 1960, shortly before its demolition.

A view along Carr Street, 27 January 1965. The buildings look very similar today, with the former site of the Beehive on the left.

Little Colman Street from Carr Street, with part of the *East Anglian Daily Times* and *Evening Star* offices and printing works, in 1965. Newspapers were published on this site from 1887 until 1966 when the company moved to its present site in Lower Brook Street. The company's fleet of delivery vans is lined up outside. The Eastgate shopping centre now stands on this site although the through way to Great Colman Street remains.

Carr Street from White Horse Corner, 13 February 1964. On the right is Heppells chemist shop with, beyond, Lavey's outfitters, Hawkins & Sons Ltd, cotton goods shop, and Mac Fisheries Ltd.

A dinner held by the Ipswich Gardeners Club in the Coop Hall in Carr Street, *c.* 1950.

The Old Cattle Market, 12 October 1959. This view from Cowells printing works shows the post office sorting office (centre left), and at the top of the picture the Blue Coat Boy public house, the Eastern Counties bus station and the Plough public house.

Tacket Street, 24 August 1958. The shops are Hawes & Sons, clothiers and tailors, Ward's grocery store, and the Tankard public house. All of these buildings have since been demolished.

The same row of buildings photographed from the other end of the street on the same day. The Salvation Army Citadel in the foreground was demolished in 1996.

The Buttermarket from Dial Lane, 17 March 1966. The shops on the left include R. Barrett, jewellers, Croasdale chemist, Murdoch's domestic appliances and music shop, and Cowells store.

The arch by St Matthew's Church neatly frames the demolition work in progress to clear the
tiny streets of St Matthews Church Lane, Stirling Street, Castle Street and Perth Street,
photographed on 27 April 1959. Civic Drive now takes the route of St Matthews Church Lane
and the Civic Centre car park is not far from the site of these tiny streets.

The boiler house chimney of St Matthews Baths being demolished in January 1965. This was a time of great change in this part of the town, with the new road scheme under construction, cutting through to the dock area. The muddy outline of Civic Drive and the huge underground car park, still being built at this time, are visible in the background (top left).

St Matthews Street was greatly changed by redevelopment in the 1960s. This postcard view of the street from the mid-1950s shows the junction with Berners Street (left). In the centre is the old Queen's Head public house which was demolished and replaced with a new version built close to the original site. The St Matthews Street roundabout is in the centre of this view today.

St Matthews Street, 7 November 1962. Most of the buildings on the left, including the seventeenth-century Golden Fleece Hotel, were demolished during the 1960s redevelopment of the area. The studios of BBC Radio Suffolk now stand behind the site of the Golden Fleece.

The Queen's Head Hotel, at the corner of St Matthews Street and St Matthews Church Lane, 1965. This is the view from what is now the roundabout.

St Matthews Street, looking towards Barrack Corner, in 1962. The shops which stood in front of St Matthews Baths had been demolished by this time.

St Matthews Baths also served as a hall during the winter months, with the swimming pool boarded over. Here members of the Women's Institute are holding their annual general meeting on 15 March 1966.

Demolition work under way in Argyle Street in the late 1950s to clear the site for the building of Wells Court flats.

The demolition of the Crown and Sceptre public house at the corner of Crown Street and High Street, 27 July 1961. Next to the pub is Graves' butchers shop and beyond that Wilcox's tobacconist and confectioner.

A police officer taking details at the scene of an accident in Cecilia Street, 17 October 1952.

Ma Minter's shop in St Helens Street was a wonderful example of the type of small shop that sold 'everything'. Close inspection shows Hacks cough sweets, cigarettes, sweet drinks, peas, chocolates, tins of soup, and much more.

Minter's shop was part of this row which was demolished to make way for Wells Court flats.

St Helens Street, from the crossroads of Grimwade Street and Argyle Street, in the 1950s. These shops were also demolished to make way for Wells Court flats. They included (from the left) G. Deeks, estate agent and house furnisher, F.J. Ansell, radio engineer, King and Waters, opticians, S.R. Ilott, greengrocer, and Bartlett's hairdressers.

The Bond Street fire station, which used to house horse-drawn steam fire pumps, closed when the new fire station opened in Princes Street.

These photographs show Colonel Hardy addressing the residents of Wells Street in the 1950s. He was there to inform them about the plans to redevelop the street. A table complete with cloth was set out for him in the middle of the street and the residents listened carefully to his announcement.

Wells Street, with its tiny terraced houses.

All gone – the demolition of Wells Street is complete. St Helens School is on the right.

These fine houses in Foundation Street were demolished in the mid-1960s and a multi-storey car park now stands on the site.

Wingfield Street, 29 November 1962. The Phoenix public house stands at the corner. All this area was cleared to make way for a multi-storey car park.

The demolition of houses in White Elm Street, 16 January 1959.

Great Whip Street, with Felaw Street off to the right, in the 1950s. The sign on the side of Haward's bakers shop on the right directs passengers to the *River Lady*.

Heavy summer rain caused flooding in Ranelagh Road in June 1958. The engineering works of Reavell and Company Ltd is on the left.

Wherstead Road was flooded in another summer storm in July 1963.

Winter snow being cleared by an Ipswich Council Highways Department snow plough in the early 1960s. Egerton's garage used to dominate this part of Crown Street but its site is now occupied by Crown Pools.

Westgate Street looking towards the Cornhill, 27 January 1965. At this time traffic flowed through what is now a pedestrianized area. The businesses on the left were John Collier, tailors, Stones television and radio, the Crown and Anchor Hotel, and Footman & Pretty's general store. On the right were the Oriental Restaurant, W.H. Smith, Paige Gowns, costumiers, Smith & Sons, cleaners, and Dolcis shoe shop. The union flag was flying at half-mast as a mark of respect following the death of Sir Winston Churchill three days earlier.

Westgate Street during the 1950s. This is the reverse view to the picture shown opposite. Halfway along on the right, at the corner of Providence Street, was the 'Fifty Shilling' tailors shop. The name of this shop gives an indication as to values at the time.

The Christmas lights in Westgate Street, 1964.

Princes Street, looking towards the town centre, September 1960. All these buildings have since been demolished. Today, the roundabout linking Franciscan Way and Civic Drive is in the centre of this view. On the right is Latimer's garage and the Friars Inn on the corner of Portman Street.

The mid-1960s saw huge changes in this part of Princes Street. The Greyfriars development was under construction as the old buildings in the area were demolished, including Spurling's auctioneers and Latimer's garage.

The Corn Exchange in operation, 26 February 1957. This building was also the home of the produce market until it moved to the Greyfriars development in the mid-1960s.

Road traffic was often brought to a standstill as railway trucks were moved across the road to and from the dock area near Stoke Bridge. This steam tram engine, on shunting duties, was photographed in operation on 1 March 1952.

Queen Elizabeth II's Coronation Day, 2 June 1953, saw celebrations all over town, despite the poor weather. A carnival procession made its way through the town centre, watched by thousands of people who braved the weather to attend the celebrations. The procession is passing through Westgate Street.

The Coronation procession passes from Carr Street into Tavern Street.

An American-theme float mounted on a vehicle from one of the US bases, in Tavern Street.

A girls' brigade band marching through Tavern Street during the Coronation procession.

A Coronation party in James Street for residents from Edgar Street, Portman Street, and Priory Street. These tiny houses and streets were lost when the Greyfriars development was built in the mid-1960s.

The Coronation was one of the BBC's first major outside broadcast events. Although reception in Ipswich was far from good, thousands watched the event on television; for many of them it was their first experience of this relatively new medium. These elderly residents were invited to watch the set at Holywells Mansion.

Houses being demolished in Crown Street, near the junction with High Street, 15 June 1959. Every building shown here has gone, including the William Pretty factory on the right, which was demolished in the 1980s.

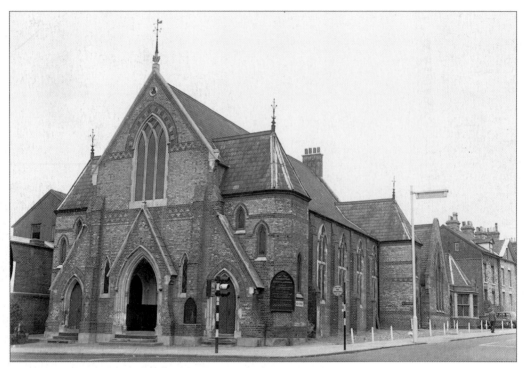

Crown Street Congregational Church at the corner of High Street, September 1964. Offices now stand on this site.

The demolition of Harmony Square in the 1950s. This was off Woodbridge Road between Lacey Street and North Hill Road.

Brewers Stuart & Patterson brought a horse-drawn dray to town as a publicity exercise on 19 August 1958. Here shoppers watch as the dray passes Ridley & Son's shop in Tavern Street.